UML for Mere Mortals® Pra

"The many sidebars in the book enliven the les_____ __._ ._.._ examples. Readers will identify with the predicaments that the authors describe from their personal experiences. They effectively demonstrate the value of the technology."

—*James Rumbaugh, Distinguished Engineer, IBM*

"In *UML for Mere Mortals*®, Maksimchuk and Naiburg promise '...just enough UML, just in time.' With such a large territory to cover, this turns out to be quite a promise, but the book carries it off with élan and polish. Sporting sufficient examples and diagrams to help the new user discover UML's value, or to help the line developer explain to his management why modeling is important, the book gets the right set of ideas across quickly and efficiently. *UML for Mere Mortals* belongs in the hands of every software developer exploring the modeling revolution, UML, and the Model Driven Architecture; and as ammunition on the bookshelf of every other developer and architect."

—*Richard Mark Soley, Chairman and CEO, Object Management Group*

"Maksimchuk and Naiburg have produced one of the liveliest and most useful 'how to' books on UML that I've seen. It is eminently readable, filled with practical advice and numerous instructive anecdotes based on their extensive field experience in applying UML in actual industrial settings. For the practitioner, this is a vade mecum to be kept within easy reach for quick reference; for the student, it is a guide that reveals the rich life hiding within the seemingly dry UML concepts."

—*Bran Selic, Distinguished Engineer, IBM Rational Software*

"A practical introduction to designing real-world business systems using UML, explained from first principles. A great book for anyone who wants to start learning the industry's standard modeling language."

—*Andrew Watson, Vice President & Technical Director, Object Management Group*

"*UML for Mere Mortals*® is an excellent guide to what the UML can do for your organization, which is clearly define projects in a standardized way, letting you reduce defects and avoid costly refactoring. It gently leads the reader through the various diagram types and modeling techniques, and is loaded with real-world anecdotes that explain how UML can help you and your team. This will be a valuable addition to the bookshelf of anyone who manages organizations, projects, or teams—or who wants to."

—*Glen Ford, President, Surpassant Software*

"If you've ever wondered what 'visual modeling' is and the role of UML in it, this is the book for you. Basics of UML are explained nicely within the context of visual modeling. Moreover, the authors enlighten you about the importance of 'modeling' in modern-day software development."

—*Ishan De Silva, Software Engineer, Millennium Information Technologies, Sri Lanka*

UML

▶ **for Mere**

▶ **Mortals** ®

Addison-Wesley presents the
For Mere Mortals® Series

Series Editor: Michael J. Hernandez

The goal of the *For Mere Mortals® Series* is to present you with information on important technology topics in an easily accessible, common-sense manner. The primary audience for *Mere Mortals* books is that of readers who have little or no background or formal training in the subject matter. Books in the Series avoid dwelling on the theoretical and instead take you right into the heart of the topic with a matter-of-fact, hands-on approach. The books are not designed to address all the intricacies of a given technology, but they do not avoid or gloss over complex, essential issues either. Instead, they focus on providing core, foundational knowledge in a way that is easy to understand and that will properly ground you in the topic. This practical approach provides you with a smooth learning curve and helps you to begin to solve your real-world problems immediately. It also prepares you for more advanced treatments of the subject matter, should you decide to pursue them, and even enables the books to serve as solid reference material for those of you with more experience. The software-independent approach taken in most books within the Series also teaches the concepts in such a way that they can be applied to whatever particular application or system you may need to use.

Titles in the Series:

Database Design for Mere Mortals®, Second Edition:
A Hands-On Guide to Relational Database Design
Michael J. Hernandez. ISBN: 0201752840

SQL Queries for Mere Mortals®:
A Hands-On Guide to Data Manipulation in SQL
Michael J. Hernandez and John L. Viescas. ISBN: 0201433362

UML for Mere Mortals®
Robert A. Maksimchuk and Eric J. Naiburg. ISBN: 0321246241

For more information, check out the series web site at
www.awprofessional.com/ForMereMortalsSeries.

UML

▶ for Mere

▶ Mortals ®

Robert A. Maksimchuk

Eric J. Naiburg

✦✦ Addison-Wesley

Boston ▪ San Francisco ▪ New York ▪ Toronto ▪ Montreal

London ▪ Munich ▪ Paris ▪ Madrid

Capetown ▪ Sydney ▪ Tokyo ▪ Singapore ▪ Mexico City

Library of Congress Publication in Data: 2004110181

Publisher: John Wait
Executive Editor: Mary O'Brien
Editorial Assistant: Brenda Mulligan
Marketing Manager: Chris Guzikowski
International Marketing Manager: Tim Galligan
Managing Editor: Gina Kanouse
Senior Project Editor: Sarah Kearns
Copy Editor: Ben Lawson
Senior Indexer: Cheryl Lenser
Proofreader: Sheri Cain
Compositor: Jake McFarland
Manufacturing Buyer: Dan Uhrig

 © 2005 by Pearson Education, Inc.

Addison-Wesley offers excellent discounts on this book when ordered in quantity for bulk purchases or special sales. For more information, please contact U.S. Corporate and Government Sales, 1-800-382-3419, corpsales@pearsontechgroup.com. For sales outside the U.S., please contact International Sales, international@pearsoned.com.

For Mere Mortals® is a registered trademark owned by Michael J. Hernandez and used with permission.

Company and product names mentioned herein are the trademarks or registered trademarks of their respective owners.

Printed in the United States of America
Third Printing: April 2005

ISBN: 0-321-24624-1

Pearson Education LTD.
Pearson Education Australia PTY, Limited.
Pearson Education Singapore, Pte. Ltd.
Pearson Education North Asia, Ltd.
Pearson Education Canada, Ltd.
Pearson Educatión de Mexico, S.A. de C.V.
Pearson Education—Japan
Pearson Education Malaysia, Pte. Ltd.

To all those I love and cherish.
—Robert A. Maksimchuk

To the loves of my life: Karalyn, Joseph, and Katherine.
—Eric J. Naiburg

Contents

Foreword   xxiii

Introduction   xxv

What Can You Expect from This Book?   xxv
  Style   xxvi

Who Should Read This Book? Read This Section!   xxvii

How to Read This Book   xxviii
  UML Versions   xxix
  Advanced Topics   xxx
  Callouts   xxx
  Paths   xxxi

CHAPTER 1   Introduction to the UML   1

What Is the Unified Modeling Language (UML)?   2
  Where Did the UML Come From?   2
  Is the UML Proprietary?   3
  Is the UML Only for Object-Oriented Development?   4
  Is the UML a Methodology?   5
  What Is Happening Now with the UML?   6

What Is a Model?   6
  Why Should I Build Models?   8
  Why Should I Model with the UML?   10
  What Can I Model with the UML?   12
  Who Should Build Models?   13

What Is a Diagram?   15
  What Diagrams Are in the UML?   15
  What Is the Difference Between Diagrams and Models?   17

Terms   18

Summary   19

Review Questions   20

CHAPTER 2   Business Models   23

What Are Business Models?   23

Why Should I Model My Business?   26

Should I Model My Entire Business?   31

How Can the UML Help Me Improve My Business?   33

How Do I Model My Business Using the UML?   34

Business Use Case Model   35
    Business Use Case Diagrams   35
    Activity Diagrams   38

Business Analysis Model   46
    Sequence Diagrams   50

Topics to Consider   55

Terms   55

Summary   56

Review Questions   56

CHAPTER 3   Requirements Modeling   59

What Are Requirements?   59

Why Bother with Requirements?   62

What Types of Requirements Are There?   63

How Can the UML Model Requirements?   64
    Review of Use Case Basics   64
    More on Use Cases   65
    Review of Sequence Diagram Basics   83
    More on Sequence Diagrams   83

Topics to Consider   85

Terms   86

Summary   86

Review Questions   87

CHAPTER 4 Architectural Modeling   89

Introduction   89

What Is Architecture?   90

Why Model Architecture?   91
   Enterprise Architecture   92
   System Architecture   93
   Software Architecture   94

Logical Architecture   94
   Class Diagrams   95
   Systems and Subsystems   99

Physical Architecture   101
   Operations   101
   Component Diagrams   102
   Deployment Diagrams   103
   Stereotypes   104

Architectural Patterns   106

What Is Model Driven Architecture?   108

Topics to Consider   109

Terms   110

Summary   110

Review Questions   111

CHAPTER 5 Application Modeling   113

Why Should I Model My Applications?   114
   Our Second Response   116
   Behind the Question   116

Should I Model My Entire Application?   117

What About Programming Languages?   119

How Deeply Should I Model My Applications?   119

How Can the UML Model Applications?   120
   Review of Class Diagram Basics   121
   More on Class Diagrams   129
   More on Sequence Diagrams   133

Topics to Consider   135

Terms   136

Summary   136

Review Questions   137

CHAPTER 6   Database Modeling   139

UML for Database Design?   139
   The Fallacy About Notations   140

How Can I Leverage UML Models Created by Others?   142
   Use Case Models   145
   Activity Models   146
   Class Models   148

What Types of Database Models Can Be Created Using the UML?   149
   Conceptual Models   149
   Logical Models   153
   Physical Models   158

Topics to Consider   161

Terms   162

Summary   162

Review Questions   163

CHAPER 7   Testing   165

How Can the UML Help Me in Testing?   165

How Can I Use the Business Use Case Models?   168
   System, Integration, and Subsystem Testing   169

How Can I Use the Business Analysis Models?   173
   Integration and Subsystem Testing   174

How Can I Use the Analysis and Design Models?   177
   Unit, Class, and Algorithmic Testing   178

What About Other Types of Testing?   181
    Performance and Regression Testing   181

Topics to Consider   182

Terms   182

Summary   183

Review Questions   184

CHAPTER 8   Is That All There Is?   187

Introduction   187

Other UML Diagrams   188
    Statechart Diagrams   188
    Collaboration Diagrams   191
    Object Diagrams   192

More on UML 2.0   193
    Changes to Collaboration Diagrams   194
    Change to Activity Diagrams   195
    Changes to Sequence Diagrams   196
    Changes to Component Diagrams   197
    Changes to Class Diagrams   199

Topics to Consider   200

Terms   200

Summary   201

Review Questions   201

CHAPTER 9   How Do I Get Started Using the UML?   203

Introduction   203

Good Beginnings   204
    The Elephant   204
    Use Cases and Risk Management   205
    Recruits   207

Growing Your Own   208
    The Training Trap   208
    Mentors   209
    Apprenticeships   210

Working Together   210
    Modeling Teams   210
    The War Room   211

Topics to Consider   212

Terms   212

Summary   212

Review Questions   213

CHAPTER 10   Where Can I Learn More?   215

Introduction   215

UML   215

Object-Oriented Analysis and Design   216

Patterns   216

Enterprise Architectures and Frameworks   217

APPENDIX A   Glossary   219

APPENDIX B   Answers to Review Questions   225

Chapter 1   Introduction to the UML   225

Chapter 2   Business Models   226

Chapter 3   Requirements Modeling   228

Chapter 4   Architectural Modeling   229

Chapter 5   Application Modeling   230

Chapter 6   Database Modeling   231

Chapter 7   Testing   231

Chapter 8   Is That All There Is?   233

Chapter 9   How Do I Get Started Using the UML?   234

APPENDIX C   UML Diagrams and Elements   235

Globally Used Elements   235

Use Case Diagram   235

Activity Diagram   236

Sequence Diagram   237

Collaboration (UML 1.x) or Communication (UML 2.0) Diagram   237

Class Diagram   238

Component Diagram   238

Deployment Diagram   239

Statechart Diagram   239

Timing Diagram   240

Index   241

Preface

Over the past 10+ years, we have been traveling the world speaking to people about modeling software, databases, businesses, and systems. This has allowed us the great pleasure of meeting thousands of people on projects, at seminars, trade shows, corporate, and government site visits. But the best part is, we have had the opportunity to learn from each and every one of them. As we and our colleagues have covered the globe through these years, many of the questions we receive are from people who just want to understand what this "UML thing" is all about and why they should bother to learn it or support it within their organization. In this book, we will return the favor by answering many of the questions we have received over these years about modeling, and specifically modeling with the Unified Modeling Language (UML).

Acknowledgments

First, thanks to God, without whose grace, none of this would have been possible.

Second, many many thanks to my family for their understanding during yet another writing project. Next, I would like to thank my co-author, Eric Naiburg, for his persistent tenacity against those difficult challenges, above and beyond the actual writing, that always seem to arise in an attempt to derail the completion of such an endeavor.

Very special thanks to Mike Engle, one of the most skilled system architects and OO practitioners I have had the pleasure to work with. His unrelenting review and commentary on this book's content was invaluable.

You may think this unusual, but upon reflection, I would like to thank the "difficult" people who I have worked with over the years. We all have these people in our lives: the people that tell you "it won't work" or "it can't be done," the nasty boss, the peer who ignores your contributions, the bureaucrats, the politicians, and so on. They give us some of our greatest challenges in life and some of our greatest blessings—they provide us with the *constructive dissonance* that keeps us dissatisfied and helps us to "move on" to the places fate intends us to be. They have no idea or intent to do us this favor, but they do. Welcome them. They are a gift. If not for them, I wouldn't be where I am at this place in time, completing my second book. To all of them, I sincerely and honestly say thank you.

—Bob Maksimchuk

I would like to first thank my co-author, Mr. Robert (Bob) Maksimchuk. Without Bob, none of this would have been possible, both from his direct contribution to this book, which is quite extensive, and his drive of both himself and me to create a high-quality, well-constructed book.

A tremendous thank you to my family. When Bob and I were writing our first book, my daughter Katherine was just on the way; now she has spent time sitting on my lap while writing this book, along with my son Joseph. Thanks to my loving wife Karalyn, without whom I wouldn't be where I am today, for her support and for keeping the children out of the way when needed.

—Eric Naiburg

We would both like to thank Mary O'Brien, Audrey Doyle, Brenda Mulligan, Gina Kanouse, Sarah Kearns, Ben Lawson, and the rest of the Addison-Wesley team and Mike Hernandez for working with us on the development of this book. Thanks to all our reviewers for keeping us grounded with their reviews and comments. Also, thanks to the numerous members of the worldwide field organization of Rational Software who have allowed us to learn from them and their clients.

And a special thank you to both Dr. Alan Brown and Grady Booch.

About the Authors

Robert A. Maksimchuk

Robert A. Maksimchuk is a veteran systems engineer with over 25 years of hardware and software systems development experience in a widely diverse group of industries. For most of his career, Mr. Maksimchuk's focus has been using his object-oriented (OO) expertise to help numerous companies employ OO techniques to solve their business problems. He is co-author of *UML for Database Design* (ISBN 0-201-72163-5), and has also written articles for various trade magazines. Mr. Maksimchuk, Industry Solutions Market Manager for IBM Rational, has traveled worldwide, speaking at numerous technology forums, companies, and conferences and leading workshops and seminars on OO development with UML.

Eric J. Naiburg

Eric J. Naiburg is group market manager of desktop products for IBM Rational Software. He is responsible for market strategy, planning, and messaging around Rational's desktop products including XDE, WebSphere Studio, Rational's testing solutions, and more. Prior to his current position, Mr. Naiburg was manager of product management, focusing on the IBM Rational Rose and IBM Rational XDE product lines. His focus was to extend the ability of Rational's products to support database design and e-business solutions within the visual modeling tools space and the UML. Mr. Naiburg came to Rational from Logic Works Inc., where he was product manager for ERwin and ModelMart. He is co-author of *UML for Database Design* (ISBN 0-201-72163-5), and has also written articles for various trade magazines.

Foreword

It's been a tough few years for the software industry. We're all being asked to do more with less, to cut back on new investments, to derive greater value from existing solutions, to be more innovative in how we address challenges. And yet as the sophistication of the applications we are asked to create increases, the complexity of the systems we need to understand, extend, and build continues to grow. How can we address these competing forces?

A key part of the answer lies in reducing the overhead associated with capturing an understanding of the problem domain that can be shared by all stakeholders, transforming that problem description into viable architectural alternatives, evaluating the range of solutions against meaningful design and operating criteria, and automating the realization of a specific solution in the technologies in use by the organization. All of these rely on a common set of techniques and approaches for software practitioners based on a language that is sufficiently rich that it can be applied to many different situations, but that can be customized to address specific concerns and not just general ones. The Unified Modeling Language (UML) offers the software industry's primary example of such a language. It embodies the best ideas from creating all kinds of system and software solutions over the past two decades, and has evolved with input from many of the most insightful people in the software industry.

However, underlying the scope, breadth, and rich heritage of the UML is a significant concern—how do we make the UML accessible to the very wide community of software professionals who can benefit from application of its concepts, notations, and semantics? Of course, a vast array of materials on UML is readily available, as a trip to any neighborhood or online book store will attest. While they contain a lot of excellent material, there has been a major hole in the kinds of information they provide. What most people require is the essential information about modeling in UML in an easily digested, no-nonsense form. They want the "spirit of UML," with the basic notational conventions in the context of what it means to apply them in practice to problems that are meaningful to them. Well, help is on its way!

I've been fortunate to work with Bob and Eric for a number of years at Rational. I know how effective they can be in cutting through the extraneous aspects of any issue to get to the heart of the matter. I've relied on their experience and insights on many occasions. I am delighted to see the same precision and intelligence is offered in *UML for Mere Mortals*®!

This book fills a significant need in the market for those looking to understand the basic ideas of UML. However, more than simply describing the notation, this book provides guidance on the application of the UML to support the primary tasks of system and software development—the kinds of things we all face every day working with our colleagues to create better software faster. In this material, Bob and Eric have managed to capture key system and software design techniques in a style that is refreshingly straightforward to understand and apply, and to distill their ideas and insight from more than a decade of practical use of UML into a book that will increase your appreciation for UML and make you more effective.

Dr. Alan W. Brown
IBM Distinguished Engineer
IBM Rational

Introduction

Topics Covered in This Introduction

What Can You Expect from This Book?

    Goals

    Style

Who Should Read This Book? Read This Section!

How to Read This Book

    UML Coverage

    UML Versions

    Advanced Topics

    Callouts

    Paths

What Can You Expect from This Book?

Goals

A better way to answer this question is to tell you first why we wrote this book. After all, a host of UML books are on the bookstore shelves now. So why did we decide to write yet another one?

Over the years, we have spoken with thousands of individuals from hundreds of companies around the world, and we learned from them that the average person involved in software development projects, even if he or she has a technical background, often sees the UML as unapproachable. People view it as so large and complex a subject that they do not have enough time to learn it. The typical UML book reinforces their beliefs because it usually incorporates numerous complex diagrams with long explanations of cryptic notations, not unlike a typical computer programming language manual. This turns off most people, except for the most passionate modelers.

Another important fact that became apparent is that most people who play a role in the software development process generally do not model on a regular basis, a fact that most UML books ignore. So, in *UML For Mere Mortals*®, we will focus on how the UML addresses the audience's needs, not UML modeling for its own sake.

Here are our goals for this book:

1. To **introduce the UML** to those technical and non-technical people who are stakeholders in software development projects but who are **not hard-core modelers**.
2. To do so in a manner that is **easy to understand**, addressing the core concepts of the UML that all mere mortals need to know.
3. To address the UML in terms of the **specific concerns of these readers**.
4. To explain the use of the UML in a **pragmatic** fashion, not in a theoretical, purist manner.
5. To use our **real-world experiences** to focus on what readers will run into on **real-world projects**.

If these goals align with your needs, this is the book for you.

Style

This book is written in a different style and organized differently from most UML texts. Most books take a "structural" approach to introducing UML, organizing the chapters by diagram type. Within the chapter, they explain all the details of each element you might find on those diagrams. This is fine for a component-by-component learning style. However, we take a "user-centric" approach, presenting the UML within a context that is relevant to a particular reader's role and the activities that that reader needs to perform on the job.

The chapters in this book are organized by major activities people perform on development projects. Then, we present the UML elements that are most useful in those activities, to the level and depth that is appropriate for those activities. In this manner, you can learn enough of the UML for the role you play in digestible chunks.

This organization creates an interesting side effect. Because a number of the UML elements are used in more than one development activity, these elements might appear in more than one chapter. Although this might appear redundant, the later chapters will typically reintroduce the topic and then discuss the specific UML elements in more detail or discuss the different way they are used for that activity. Thus, you can learn the basics about an element in an early chapter, and if that's all you need or want, that is fine. If you want to learn more details, you will find them in a subsequent chapter. In addition, revisiting a topic in a subsequent chapter will help reinforce the basic UML concepts for you.

Who Should Read This Book? Read This Section!

Please do not overlook this section. You only have so much time and money to invest in expanding your professional knowledge. We're sure you don't want to spend those precious personal resources on things that don't help you. This is why it is so important to read this section of any book you are considering for purchase. Obviously, we would like our readers to have a positive experience with this book. We want this book to meet your needs.

As mentioned before, the main audience for this book can be described as people who play a role in the software development process but who generally do not model on a regular basis. These people are not the avid software modelers who develop models routinely. Some examples of the primary readers of this book are as follows:

1. Business people who are responsible for improving their business's market position and are using software development as a key component in addressing the business goals.

2. Business analysts who are responsible for creating system requirements to address the needs of the business.

3. Software architects and designers who do not know the UML but who need to build flexible, resilient systems and want to start specifying these systems with the UML.

4. Development managers and team leaders who are involved with or responsible for executing successful software development projects.

5. Programmers who do not know the UML but who must implement the software designs that they receive, which are expressed in the UML.

6. Database designers who work with teams using the UML or who want to learn the basics about UML in general and UML for database design.

7. Educators who want to or are teaching introductory UML classes.

8. Technical writers who need to translate UML-based specifications into documentation.

9. Anyone whom the boss asks to teach him or her about the UML. Just hand the boss this book and go back to work.

If you find yourself in one of these groups, or something similar, we believe this book will meet your expectations. (Just to make sure, if you haven't read the previous section, "What Can You Expect from This Book?," please do so.) When we meet you at a conference or at your company, we'd love to hear about your positive experiences with this material.

In summary, this book is intended **for the person who is fairly new to the UML** and would like to understand what UML is about, where it fits in their job environment, and **how to understand the models they receive from others** in their workplace. **It is not intended to teach the entire UML,** nor is it our plan to teach the process of object-oriented analysis and design or software development. As the title of this book indicates (*UML for Mere Mortals*), it is for the person who might not be an experienced software architect or expert designer, but who is part of the other 80% of the development community who just have a need or will to understand a bit more.

How to Read This Book

UML Coverage

This book is structured to give you just enough UML, just in time. As we said earlier, this book is not intended to show you every nook and cranny of every UML element. Plenty of large, thick, thrilling UML manuals are out there for that purpose—definitely not for mere mortals.

One of the major truths that the practitioners we have talked to have validated is that nobody uses the entire UML. Just as studies have shown that the average English-speaking person uses less than 3,000 words of the English language, most people use less than half the diagrams in the UML. We want to give you enough information on the parts of the UML that you will see most often.

To that end, most of the content of this book focuses on those areas of the UML that you are most likely to run into on development projects. Those will be the areas that our real-world customers have told us they use most frequently. These key areas will get most of the coverage because they will be the most useful to you. We will also cover other areas of the UML, just in less depth.

UML Versions

At the time of this writing, the latest fully approved version is UML 1.5. That being said, UML 2.0 is working its way through the final approval process. The formal and final approval is expected this year. Keep the following in mind, even after UML 2.0 is formally released:

1. Most of the existing UML models you will be working with for the time being will be UML 1.5 (or even 1.4). Most people won't change over to UML 2.0 immediately. (They will be in the middle of an ongoing projects using an earlier version, or they won't roll out new UML 2.0 modeling tools mid-project, or they will stay with their current version until they learn UML 2.0, and so forth.)

2. When discussing their models, people will still use the earlier UML terminology for some time because they have used it for years, so you will need to be familiar with both versions because of both this and the previous reason.

3. Only about 25% of the new changes in UML 2.0 will be seen by users. (Most of the changes are to the "infrastructure" and are not visible to the end users.)

4. Most modeling practitioners (non-mere mortals) use only a small portion of the UML. Thus, it can be expected that mere mortals will use even less. A mere mortal might encounter only a few of the UML 2.0 changes.

Because of these reasons, we decided to address the new version changes in a pragmatic manner. Where there is a change in the diagrams between UML 1.5 and 2.0, and **where those changes are relevant to mere mortals**, the text will introduce the concepts using UML 1.5 and will note any significant change for UML 2.0. Subsequently, in a later chapter that discusses UML 2.0, those changes that are most important to mere mortals will be addressed more fully.

Advanced Topics

Along with introducing the UML basics and answering the most common questions on a given UML topic, most chapters have a "Topics to Consider" section. This section simply introduces some of the more advanced considerations on a given UML topic, without further elaboration. If you have the desire to go deeper in a given topic, these are the areas where you can start. In other words, these are areas "for the interested student" to pursue on his or her own with the aid of an advanced text or experienced mentor. You might want to begin with some of the selected resources cited in Chapter 10 and at the end of each chapter.

Callouts

While reading, you will encounter other artifacts in this book. There are various types of "callouts" or sidebars throughout the chapters. First are the Deep Dive callouts, indicated by the preceding icon. While this is a book for mere mortals, there are some more in depth topics that you will need to know about. They are important because it is likely you will run into them in practice.

This brings us to the next type—the Real World callout identified with the preceding icon. People always want to know more about what other people in the industry are doing in general and what they are doing with the UML. The Real World callouts are intended to bring you the experiences that we, our colleagues, or other people have had working for various companies on real-world projects.

Because these real experiences enable all of us to learn from the problems real practitioners have experienced, we have an obligation to try not to embarrass anyone. So we have omitted company names and locations, written the stories in the first person, and elided some of the details to protect the innocent (and sometimes the not-so innocent).

You will also see a Lessons Learned icon to give you quick access to important takeaways (often associated with the Real World experiences).

The last type of callout is the Watch Out callout marked with the preceding icon. These discuss the pitfalls people often run into that you want to avoid.

Paths

You can take various paths when reading this book:

1. If you are brand new to the UML and modeling, simply read the book linearly. Pay particular attention to Chapter 9 and do all the review questions.

2. If you just want an overview of the most often seen UML topics, read Chapters 2 through 6. You might want to skip the Deep Dives and the Topics to Consider sections. You should also reinforce what you learn by answering all the review questions. This should help you enough so that you will not be completely lost if someone puts a UML diagram in front of you.

3. If you want to be able to contribute (as a mere mortal) to modeling discussions when a UML design is presented to you, read Chapters 2 through 8, paying close attention to all the callouts and review questions, and even take the time to do some self-study on the Topics to Consider that are appropriate to your situation (the references in Chapter 10 can help you here).

4. If you need to "bootstrap" yourself on a particular area of modeling, say, modeling an architecture or modeling requirements, go to that particular chapter. This might require you to cross-reference other areas of the text.

5. If you are a modeling practitioner who already knows the basics, you might want to sharpen some of your skills by focusing on the Deep Dive, Real World, and Watch Out areas and exploring the Topics to Consider. You might also want to fully read the chapters covering the areas where you might not have experience using the UML, for example, using UML for database design or for business modeling.

However you choose to approach this book, we hope you enjoy it.

1

Introduction to the UML

Topics Covered in This Chapter

What Is the Unified Modeling Language (UML)?

    Where Did the UML Come From?

    Is the UML Proprietary?

    Is the UML Only for Object-Oriented Development?

    Is the UML a Methodology?

    What Is Happening Now with the UML?

What Is a Model?

    Why Should I Build Models?

    Why Should I Model with the UML?

    What Can I Model with the UML?

    Who Should Build Models?

What Is a Diagram?

    What Diagrams Are in the UML?

    What Is the Difference Between Diagrams and Models?

Terms

Summary

Review Questions

What Is the Unified Modeling Language (UML)?

The Unified Modeling Language (UML) is the standard visual modeling language used for modeling businesses, software applications, and system architectures. Although the UML is a standard of the Object Management Group (OMG—http://www.omg.org/), the UML is not just for modeling object-oriented (OO) software applications. The UML is a graphical language that was designed to be very flexible and customizable. This enables you to create many different types of models, including models for understanding business processes, workflow, sequences of queries, applications, databases, architectures, and more.

Where Did the UML Come From?

To understand the UML, it helps to know its origins. During the late 1980s and into the 1990s, many object-oriented modeling techniques were being developed to model software. Because different people developed these approaches using different visual modeling techniques and notations, the world of application modeling was becoming divided. To further complicate matters, some techniques were designed just for application modeling, and others were targeted at specific areas such as database design. Some leveraged the strengths of the others, but some remained distinct.

Three of these methodologies began to lead the pack in the marketplace. While working for General Electric, Jim Rumbaugh created the Object Modeling Technique (OMT). Ivar Jacobson developed his Object-Oriented Software Engineering method (a.k.a. the Objectory Method), primarily supporting the telecommunicationsindustry in Sweden. Grady Booch developed the self-named Booch Method. Each had their strengths and weaknesses, and each had somewhat different followings.

In the mid 1990s, Rational Software hired Jim Rumbaugh to join Grady Booch and combine their modeling methods into what became version 0.8, the first public draft of what was then called the Unified Method. In 1995, Jacobson joined Rumbaugh and Booch at Rational. Together, they developed version 0.9 of the Unified Method in 1996. Other companies joined Booch, Rumbaugh, and Jacobson as part of the UML Consortium. In 1997, they submitted version 1.0 of the Unified Method—renamed as the Unified Modeling Language, or UML—to the OMG. As an independent standards body, the OMG took over the UML development and released subsequent versions of the UML (see Figure 1-1). This year (2004), the final approval of the latest version, UML 2.0, is expected.

What makes the UML different from the independent notations we mentioned earlier is that the UML is the creation not of just Booch, Rumbaugh, and Jacobson, but also of many industry experts, software development tool companies, corporate software development organizations, and others. So began the worldwide standard modeling language of software development.

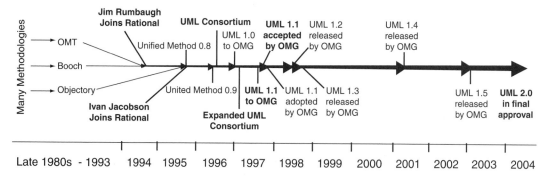

Figure 1-1 *History of the UML.*

Is the UML Proprietary?

As you decide whether to use the UML to model, one of the main things you need to consider is whether other people who join your organization will be able to understand what you have done and whether it will be communicated unambiguously. Both are good reasons for wanting to select a modeling language that is in the public domain and that is understood around the world.

As we discussed earlier in this chapter, the UML was designed because the different modeling languages that were available at the time were leading to a divergence in the ways to model. However, bringing the three major methods together wasn't quite enough. That is why Rational sought out the involvement of organizations such as IBM, Oracle, Platinum Technologies, and many others to be UML partners in the creation of the UML. They then handed development to the OMG to ensure that the UML would become a standard.

As a result, the UML is *not* proprietary. It is an open modeling standard designed and supported by software companies, consultants, other corporations, and governments who need and rely on this standard.

Although a standard open language is critical to protect you from being locked in by the whims of a technology vendor, having a modeling language that is flexible also is key. As technologies and businesses change, so does the way you model. The UML has conventions built into it that enable you to customize it as needed. These customized versions are created using "stereotypes." You will learn more about them in Chapter 5, "Application Modeling."

Is the UML Only for Object-Oriented Development?

We travel the world talking about modeling and the UML. When we begin to discuss using the UML for business or data modeling (both of which we cover in later chapters), one of the first questions we hear is, "How would I use the UML for that? Isn't it only for object-oriented development?" This is one of the biggest myths we run across. The myth comes from the reality that the UML was devised to satisfy the need to model object-oriented systems and to enable Component-Based Development (CBD). In an OO system, generally several components are tied together using what are called "interfaces." To understand how those different components interact, it is quite useful to build a model.

Although the UML was originally built for this cause, it also was built with other needs in mind. Grady Booch once told us that when he and his colleagues were designing the UML, they based a lot of what they did on the different database modeling techniques already being used in the industry. Similarly, one of the strengths of Jacobson's Objectory Method was its business modeling capability. So when they added elements of Jacobson's Objectory Method to the UML mix, they added business modeling to UML.

Today, you can model almost anything you want to in the UML by using its built-in extension and customization capabilities. The UML features an underlying meta-model (see the "Deep Dive" sidebar on meta-models later in this chapter) that enables the UML to be flexible enough so that you can do what you need to do with it. We have seen the UML used for modeling businesses, data, organizations, theoretical political systems, legal contracts, biological systems, languages, hardware, non-object-oriented application modeling such as COBOL, and many other modeling tasks.

Is the UML a Methodology?

Methodology:

> "Methodology n.
>
> **1a.** A body of practices, procedures, and rules used by those who work in a discipline or engage in an inquiry; a set of working methods: *the methodology of genetic studies; a poll marred by faulty methodology.*
>
> **b.** The study or theoretical analysis of such working methods.
>
> **2.** The branch of logic that deals with the general principles of the formation of knowledge.
>
> **3.** *Usage Problem…*
>
> *Methodology* can properly refer to the theoretical analysis of the methods appropriate to a field of study or to the body of methods and principles particular to a branch of knowledge. … In recent years, however, *methodology* has been increasingly used as a pretentious substitute for *method* in scientific and technical contexts, as in *The oil company has not yet decided on a methodology for restoring the beaches*. … But the misuse of *methodology* obscures an important conceptual distinction between the tools of scientific investigation (properly *methods*) and the principles that determine how such tools are deployed and interpreted."
> [AMER1]

This very typical definition of the term *methodology* explains that a methodology is much more than a language. You can see from the "usage problem" discussed in this definition how this can confuse some people who are new to the UML. The UML is a language. Object-oriented analysis and design (OOAD) is a process, governed by specific practices. Although languages, including the UML, have rules for syntax and usage, they do not have procedures (i.e., processes) or practices. A methodology must include these things as well. So, although a common language is needed in a specific discipline, language alone does not make a methodology. This is true for the UML as well. Thus, you can use the UML with various methodologies, but it is not a methodology itself.

What Is Happening Now with the UML?

As of this writing, the UML is in the final stages of approval for its latest revision, version 2.0. The OMG has been developing this version of the UML for many years. It combines the efforts of more than 100 organizations, bringing together the best practices they developed over the first few versions of the UML as well as needs they identified for the future.

Along with enhancing the UML infrastructure, adding new modeling capabilities, and enabling the easier exchange of models (i.e., between tools or systems), one of the OMG's main goals when developing UML 2.0 was to make it more extensible to accommodate present as well as future needs. For example, one long-standing need that is being addressed is the use of the UML to model embedded systems. (Unlike general-purpose systems such as desktop computers, embedded systems are special-purpose systems such as pacemakers, automotive braking systems, digital cameras, cruise missiles, mobile phones, and so forth that contain hardware and software designed to perform specific functions.) Typically, you would model embedded systems using different languages. But in the on-demand world of today, where you need to link your embedded systems with business systems in your organization, you need to understand how everything works together. This is greatly simplified if you model everything in the same language because it enables you to share information across different types of technologies and different modeling efforts. Prior to version 2.0, the UML provided some of this capability, but the additions the OMG made to the language in version 2.0 have greatly increased this capability.

What Is a Model?

Good question.

Model:

1. A miniature representation of an object.
2. A pattern on which something not yet produced will be based.
3. A design or type.
4. One serving as an example to be emulated or imitated.

Modeling:

   1. To construct a plan, esp. after a pattern. [WEBS1]

You are surrounded by models every day. As you get ready for work in the morning, you turn on your television. The morning news presents the local weather map showing how rain will be moving in this weekend. You reach for your vitamins. The cap is imprinted with a diagram showing how to remove the child-proof (or should we say adult-proof) cap.

You complete your morning ritual and jump into your automobile for the always-pleasant commute to the office. You stop to pick up some breakfast. You notice that behind the counter is a laminated poster containing a series of pictures (no words) showing the fast-food staff how to assemble your breakfast sandwich. Then, back on the road you go.

Half way to the office, you hear a traffic report of an accident ahead, so you pull off the road and consult your road atlas for an alternate route. You stay alert for the overhead highway signs with the large arrows indicating the lanes of traffic and which lane turns into the alternate exit you are searching for. You arrive at the office. As you stroll through the lobby, you see the glass-enclosed 3D replica of the new corporate headquarters that is under construction. You make it to your cubicle just in time to attend a morning meeting where a benefits person is showing bar charts of how much your money can earn if you invest it in the company retirement plan.

The weather map (a model or representation of the weather), the child-proof cap (a process model of how to remove the cap), the laminated sandwich instructions (another process model), the road atlas (an abstracted model of the road), the highway sign (a directional model of the highway), the corporate headquarters replica (a physical model of the building and surrounding terrain), and the bar chart (an analytical model) all model various aspects of your world.

A model, in the sense that we will discuss in this book, is a visual way of depicting your business, its rules, the use of your systems, applications, and system architectures, and interactions within your systems. You might have seen this described as "visual modeling," a term made popular by many computer-aided software engineering (CASE) vendors over the past couple of decades. Because models don't necessarily have to be visual (they can be textual or mathematical, for example, as we saw earlier), visual modeling has come to describe exactly what it implies: models that are visual in nature, using specific graphical representations.

In the remainder of this chapter, you will learn about the value of modeling, specifically when designing software and applications. First, you will learn why models should be built and then who should be building those models. We also introduce the different types of UML models that you can build.

Why Should I Build Models?

One of the most frequent objections to the UML we have heard isn't about the UML itself; it's that some people believe that there is no value in modeling. One theme you will pick up throughout this book is that modeling for modeling's sake is of little value, but when you do it for the right reasons, modeling is quite valuable. Modeling helps you to communicate designs, quickly clarify complex problems and scenarios, and ensure that your designs come closer to reality prior to implementation. This can save you and your organization a lot of time and money, and it enables teams of people (be they teams of 2 or 2,000) to work together more effectively and ensure that they are working toward the same common goals.

Think of it this way. Would you build a house without a plan? You might not build a small-scale version of the house first, but you (or your architect and builder) certainly would have design sketches, architecture drawings, and engineering assessments in hand prior to starting construction.

From the Real World—Houses Are Similar to Software

Before embarking on my software development career, I spent several years building houses. During that time, I learned that when you use a good model (design), the house will stand through time and different weather conditions and will be amicable to changes that might be needed later, such as adding a window. If you don't use a good model but instead use a design you have in your mind, there is a good chance your final product won't be what you intended.

Designing software brings similar challenges. You need to ensure that the designs and plans are eventually realized and realized correctly so that they last architecturally through time, and you must also ensure that if you do need to make changes, they too can endure over time. Also, you need to understand what changes will break your design. When you add a window to a house, for instance, you need to know where the pipes and wires are and what types of support exist to handle the load. Likewise, when you add a component to a system, you need to make sure the system won't come crashing down as a result.

Lessons Learned

1. Design so that you can accommodate unplanned changes.
2. Create a well-documented design so that others who are new to the design can still work with it.
3. Have a visual model of an architecture to help you determine implications of change.

Watch Out

Do not model for modeling's sake. Make your models actionable so that users understand why you created the models and what you expect should result from them in the future.

Also, be warned! Watch out for "analysis paralysis." This occurs when you spend too much time analyzing a problem and don't get to the point where you are being productive.

When you focus on making your analysis or modeling actionable, you set a plan as to what you want to achieve from your analysis. You also adopt a mindset to approach modeling without rushing, making it of value, and then moving on to the next thing—be it another model, a change to the business or business process, or something else such as writing code.

Another reason you should model is simply to understand your business and its processes. You model your business processes not only to understand what the business does and how it functions but also so that you can identify how changes will affect the business. Modeling the business helps you to identify strengths and weaknesses, identify areas that need to be changed or optimized, and in some cases, simulate different business process options.

Why Should I Model with the UML?

When we explain why people should model with the UML, we like to draw a parallel to the field of electrical engineering. Electrical engineers draw a schematic for an electrical device in a standard way (see Figure 1-2), using a common visualization so that no matter where you are in the world, the schematic is always interpreted in the same way. Anyone who is trained in reading such a diagram can easily understand the circuit design and how the device will function. Even those who might not be experts but who understand the symbols can still understand what part belongs where and how they are connected.

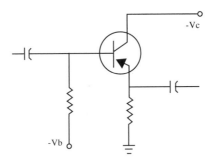

Figure 1-2 *An electrical schematic.*

Other walks of life have similar languages or notations that are specific to their disciplines. The field of music, for instance, has a standard notation (see Figure 1-3). This was a critical development in the musical field. Before this notation was developed, the only way a composer could correctly and consistently teach musicians how to play his music was in person (a conundrum that closely parallels the software industry before the development of the UML).

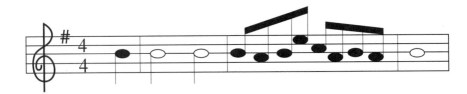

Figure 1-3 *Musical notation.*

Similarly, mathematics has its own specific notation (see Figure 1-4). In fact, the language of mathematics is often cited as the one common language that all advanced civilizations understand.

$$F(z) = [1/(2\pi)^{0.5}] \int_{-\infty}^{z} e^{-(\frac{1}{2})t^2} dt$$

Figure 1-4 *Mathematical notation.*

The same is true for the UML. It provides a common "language" to bring together business analysts, software developers, architects, testers, database designers, and the many other professionals who are involved in software design and development so that they can understand the business, its requirements, and how the software and architectures will be created. Although a cellist might not understand how to play the trumpet, she will understand what notes a trumpeter plays and when because she understands musical notation. Similarly, a business analyst who knows the UML can understand what a programmer is creating using the UML because the UML is a common language. With the ongoing need to think globally when building software, the ability provided by the UML to communicate globally becomes very important.

From the Real World—Not Lost in Translation

We were recently working with a large financial institution. They began to outsource much of their software development for a specific project. In an effort to keep costs low, they chose a well-respected international systems integrator to run the job, but they also wanted to maintain control of the system that was being built, so they kept their own architects on the project. Because the company developed the system in this way, rather than doing everything themselves, senior management had the comfort of knowing that the project would fulfill the specified requirements while staying within budget and time constraints

The financial institution had the people who understood their business. They had the domain expertise and the contacts within the business to gather and verify the requirements as needed. Their initial concerns

continues

From the Real World—Not Lost in Translation (*continued*)

centered on the ability to transfer information between the different organizations and across international borders. That information had to be well understood and couldn't be allowed to slow down the process. Understanding this prior to the request for proposal, the financial institution included that the contractor must use a UML-based modeling tool and follow specific quality processes as part of their contract. They found quickly that having a common language to interpret requirements and architectures enabled them to understand each other without having to translate designs and desires.

Lessons Learned

1. Having a common way to understand what needs to be built helped this team of different organizations, languages, and countries communicate effectively to successfully deliver an application that was on time and, more importantly, that met the requirements of their end users.

What Can I Model with the UML?

The UML enables you to model many different facets of your business, from the actual business and its processes to IT functions such as database design, application architectures, hardware designs, and much more. Designing software and systems is a complicated task requiring the coordinated efforts of different groups performing various functions: capturing the needs of the business and systems, bringing software components together, constructing databases, assembling hardware to support the systems, and so on.

You can use the different types of UML diagrams (summarized later in this chapter) to create various types of models. Figure 1-5 lists these models and their usage. The models are composed of different diagram types, model elements, and linkages between model elements that enable you to trace between them so that you can understand how they relate. Different people in the organization use these models to describe different information. As we continue throughout this book, we will elaborate on these models, their use, and the roles of the people who will be using these models.

Model Type	Model Usage
Business	Business processes, workflow, organization
Requirements	Requirements capture and communication
Architecture	High-level understanding of the system being built, interaction between different software systems, communicate system designs to developers
Application	Architecture of the lower-level designs inside the system itself
Database	Design the structures of the database and how it will interact with the application(s)

Figure 1-5   *Model types and usage.*

Who Should Build Models?

Not everyone should be involved in building models, but that doesn't mean everyone can't take advantage of the models that are built. In software design and development, you should start with models that help you understand the business and end with models designed to test your applications (and repeat this process with each software iteration thereafter). A model should be a living item that continues to be updated as the business and system are updated. The model should provide understanding, communication, and direction. If it isn't updated throughout the entire software development process, it can become stale and useless, so it's imperative that your organization has a process for dealing with models and with overall model development that includes who should be creating, updating, and maintaining the models over time.

Your organization also needs to take advantage of its staff as well as external resources. An organization typically has many domain experts, often in a business analyst-type role. These people would be building and designing business models of what is in place today (as is) and where the organization is heading (as desired). These experts often must build application models at the architectural level. As such, they must understand how what you are building will interact with itself (components within itself) and with other systems inside the organization. Architects also might take on this role as well.

As an application developer, writing code is what you like to do. But writing code without designing how it will interact can be dangerous to the integrity of the system, and that is why developers should also model the code before they write it. If they are using certain tools that enable code generation from the models developed, you can automate the creation of the boring code development tasks and get down to doing the fun development work of implementing business- and technology-specific code.

As a tester, you might not get involved directly in model building, but as you will learn later in this book, understanding the models can be quite useful when you have to create your tests. If testers are following an Extreme Programming (XP) style of software development process, they might also get involved in creating the models. XP proclaims that development requirements come from test cases that are created prior to the start of coding. That approach is a bit different from other processes in which test cases are created *from* requirements and aren't considered *the* requirements. This means that when testers follow an XP process, they also are really designing the requirements and thus modeling them (textually), which ensures a better understanding by everyone else involved in the development process.

From the Real World—Flying Toward Success

A large airline company I worked with had a great way of deciding who would model and how to avoid the issue of too many people modeling. The company created teams of people from different parts of the business, including information technology (IT). You might have heard the term of "two in a box," referring to putting two people with different skills together so that they can team up and leverage each other's strengths. This company put more than two people together, but they got similar results. They teamed up to design first-level models (called domain models), in which they defined different elements such as the many different types of agents involved within the airline industry and how they interacted with the different parts of the business. More than 10 different types of agents were in their organization, including travel, ticket, gate, etc. By coming together as a team, they leveraged the different types of expertise available and ensured that all constituents involved in the process agreed to both the terminology and how each agent was involved in the business process. As the book continues, we will examine other successes seen in this organization.

What Is a Diagram?

Diagram:

1. A plan, sketch, drawing, or outline designed to demonstrate or explain how something works or to clarify the relationship between the parts of a whole.

2. *Mathematics.* A graphic representation of an algebraic or geometric relationship.

3. A chart or graph. [DICT1]

For our purposes in this book, a *diagram* is the layout and visualization of different modeling elements as described within the UML. Each UML diagram is used for a specific purpose, typically to visualize a certain aspect of your system (summarized next). Each diagram uses specific UML symbols to achieve its purpose.

What Diagrams Are in the UML?

The UML contains two different basic diagram types: structure diagrams and behavior diagrams. Structure diagrams depict the static structure of the elements in your system. The various structure diagrams are as follows:

- **Class diagrams** are the most common diagrams used in UML modeling. They represent the static things that exist in your system, their structure, and their interrelationships. They are typically used to depict the logical and physical design of the system.

- **Component diagrams** show the organization and dependencies among a set of components. They show a system as it is implemented and how the pieces inside the system work together.

- **Object diagrams** show the relationships between a set of objects in the system. They show a snapshot of the system at a point in time.

- **Deployment diagrams** show the physical system's runtime architecture. A deployment diagram can include a description of the hardware and the software that resides on that hardware.

UML 2.0 adds the following structure diagrams:

- **Composite structure** diagrams show the internal structure of model elements.
- **Package diagrams** depict the dependencies between packages. (A package is a model element used to group together other model elements.)

Behavior diagrams depict the dynamic behavior of the elements in your system. The various behavior diagrams are as follows:

- **Activity diagrams** show the flow of activities within a system. You often would use them to describe different business processes.
- **Use case diagrams** address the business processes that the system will implement. The use cases describe ways the system will work and who will interact with it. [BOOCH1]
- **Statechart diagrams** show the state of an object and how that object transitions between states. A statechart diagram can contain states, transitions, events, and activities. A statechart diagram provides a dynamic view and is quite important when modeling event-driven behavior. For example, you could use a statechart diagram to describe a switch in a telephone routing system. That switch will change states based on different events, and you can model those events in a statechart diagram to understand how the switch behaves. In UML 2.0, these are called **state machine diagrams**.
- **Collaboration diagrams** are a type of interaction diagram, as are sequence diagrams (along with others in UML 2.0, noted next). The collaboration diagram emphasizes how objects collaborate and interact. In UML 2.0, the equivalent of the collaboration diagram is the **communication diagram**.
- **Sequence diagrams** are another type of interaction diagram. Sequence diagrams emphasize the time ordering of messages between different elements of a system.

UML 2.0 adds the following behavior diagrams:

- **Timing diagrams** are another type of interaction diagram. They depict detailed timing information and changes to state or condition information of the interacting elements.
- **Interaction overview diagrams** are high-level diagrams used to show an overview of flow of control between interaction sequences.

The UML 2.0 diagrams that are relevant to mere mortals will be discussed further in Chapter 8, "Is That All There Is?."

Although these diagrams are the defined diagrams of the UML, you may encounter additional diagrams that tool vendors can create, which are specific to their tools. You need not be concerned about the proliferation of additional UML diagrams. Few people even use all of the standard UML diagrams when modeling their systems. Some you may never use. In subsequent chapters, we will focus on those diagrams that are most important and that will most frequently be encountered by mere mortals.

What Is the Difference Between Diagrams and Models?

Although they might appear to be similar at first glance, a diagram and a model are different from each other. A model is an abstraction that contains all the elements needed to describe the intention of the thing being modeled. This can include all aspects concerning the business, systems, relationships, and more. A diagram is a specific view into what you are trying to understand in a specific context. Diagrams are just one way of looking at all or some part of that model. You can have a specific modeling element exist only once within a model, but the same element can appear on one or more diagrams.

For example, if I am modeling a navigational system for a vehicle, the system model will represent all the parts of the entire system. However, I may create specific diagrams that contain just the elements that deal with the map display, error correction, or the navigational satellite constellations.

Deep Dive—Meta-Models

A meta-model is a model of a model. The UML meta-model expresses the proper semantics and structure for UML models. A UML model is made up of many different elements. The meta-model defines the characteristics of these elements, the ways in which these elements can be related, and what such relationships mean.

What does this mean in plain English? Let's say you want to model various types of people. All people have some common characteristics (e.g., height, weight, eye color). But people also have characteristics and behaviors that are specific to each of them. A construction worker, a dancer, and an engineer are all types of people, but they are different from each other in some ways. You can model this in the UML because the structure of the UML meta-model allows you to model relationships between specific things (construction worker, dancer, engineer) and a general thing (a person)—this is called a "generalization" relationship. In other words, the UML meta-model sets the rules for how you can model.

The UML meta-model is also the foundation for UML's extensibility. Using the definitions of UML elements in the meta-model, you can create new UML modeling elements. You can add additional properties to the new elements. This allows you to give the new element additional characteristics and behaviors for your specific needs, while it still remains compliant with the structure and semantics of the original element that it was based upon. In this way, users can customize the UML to their specific needs.

Most technical languages, including Structured Query Language (SQL, the relational database language) and Business Process Modeling Language (BPML), have a meta-model. Different tool vendors may alter the standard meta-model to fit their tool or to differentiate it from their competition. In this way, tool vendors take advantage of the standards but also differentiate themselves from each other through these extensions.

Terms

Unified Modeling Language	Object-oriented development
Methodology	Object Management Group
Object Modeling Technique	Booch method
Objectory method	Stereotype

Model

Meta-models

Class diagram

Component diagram

Object diagram

Statechart diagram

Analysis paralysis

Diagram

Activity diagram

Collaboration diagram

Deployment diagram

Sequence diagram

Use case diagram

Summary

In this chapter, we introduced you to the UML. You learned where it came from and how it became the standard modeling language for software development. We dispelled some myths about the UML, particularly concerning object-oriented development and methodology. You learned that the UML does not restrict you in these areas.

We then moved to a brief discussion of why modeling is important, and you learned how the UML provides a common language, just as the standard notations of other domains such as engineering and mathematics do.

We continued this chapter with a discussion of what is currently happening with the UML. There you found that the UML continues to evolve through the effort of hundreds of organizations that are driving improved support for systems and software development. Then, we provided an overview of the value of modeling as it relates to software development, while showing similarities to other types of modeling such as an architectural design of a building.

Moving toward the focus of this book, we began our discussion of the UML and what it is used for. You learned that the UML is a standard language that you can use to communicate software and system designs to keep the entire team on the same page. Although a limited number of team members might build the models, everyone involved in the software development process can use the models. Architects use models to communicate intended architectural designs, customers review business models to ensure that the modelers understand their business needs, developers review models to build the right software as designed by architects and other developers, project managers use models to understand what is being built and to manage schedules, and so forth. Testers can leverage the models to support building test cases to understand how the software is to be used, and to communicate back to the developers on things they see that aren't correct.

Toward the end of this chapter, you began to understand how the different types of elements live within the UML, including the diagram and model types, and what they are used for at a high level. Models consist of multiple diagrams, and the diagrams are a visualization of elements and how they interact with other elements. Throughout this chapter, we stressed the value of using the visualization to ensure that the team works together and shares information wherever possible to manage the success of a project.

Review Questions

1. What does the acronym "UML" stand for?

2. Who controls the UML standard?

3. True or False: The UML is a proprietary standard.

4. What type of systems can you model with the UML?

5. True or False: You can use the UML only for object-oriented development.

6. What methodology do you use when you use the UML?

7. Name three benefits to modeling with the UML.

8. Does a model have to be visual?

9. What is analysis paralysis?

10. True or False: UML models are of value to even small projects of one or two developers.

11. Name two ways to model a business.

12. What is the most commonly used UML diagram?

13. What UML diagram do you use to model workflow?

14. What diagram type do business analysts most commonly use to identify high-level business processes?

You can find the answers to these questions in Appendix B.

[AMER1] *The American Heritage® Dictionary of the English Language, Fourth Edition.* Boston: Houghton Mifflin Company, 2000.

[BOOCH1] Booch, Grady, Rumbaugh, James, and Jacobson, Ivar. *The Unified Modeling Language User Guide.* Reading, MA: Addison-Wesley Longman, Inc., 1999.

[DICT1] http://dictionary.reference.com/.

[WEBS1] *Webster's II New Riverside Desk Dictionary.* 1988.

Business Models

Topics Covered in This Chapter

What Are Business Models?

Why Should I Model My Business?

Should I Model My Entire Business?

How Can the UML Help Me Improve My Business?

How Do I Model My Business Using the UML?

Business Use Case Model

    Business Use Case Diagrams

    Activity Diagrams

Business Analysis Model

    Business Objects Diagrams

    Sequence Diagrams

Topics to Consider

Terms

Summary

Review Questions

What Are Business Models?

Simply put, a business model is an abstract representation of a business that provides a simplified look at various aspects of the business. A business isn't represented with just one type of "business model." Different models will emphasize certain business characteristics or concepts while hiding other aspects at the same time. In this way, you can focus on certain relevant information about the part of the business that you want to address. For instance, we are all familiar with organization charts, which are models of a business's overall organizational and management reporting structure (see Figure 2-1).

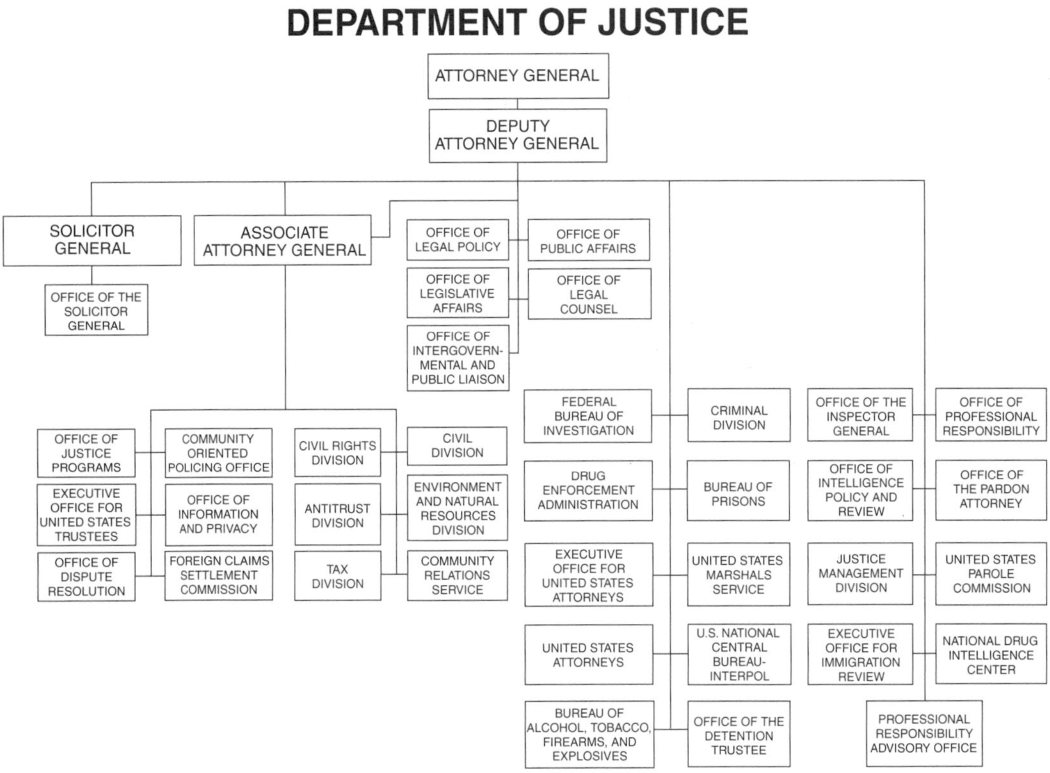

DEPARTMENT OF JUSTICE

Figure 2-1   *Business organization chart for the Department of Justice.*

There are business process models that show the flow of activities (typically within the business) that occur to perform a given business function (see Figure 2-2).

Then there are the "business models" you hear about on the financial news reports. These are "models" (typically non-visual, but they could be represented visually) that explain how a business expects to build its markets, generate revenue, and grow the business.

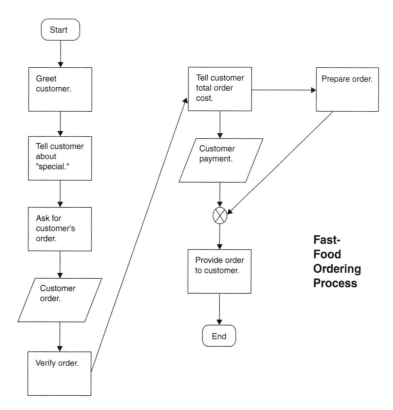

Figure 2-2   *Business process model (non-UML) showing the flow of activities in the fast-food ordering process.*

Each of these examples provides a different view of the business, similar to the construction example mentioned in Chapter 1, "Introduction to the UML." So what views do we need in our context of eventually building an information technology (IT) system? (Remember, we are not modeling just to model.) We need models that will capture the structure and interactions between the following:

- The business's organizations or departments.
- Their stakeholders—customers, workers, business partners, etc.
- The business functions that the business executes, whether for its customers or for internal purposes.
- The business assets used to fulfill the business functions.

- For geographically dispersed businesses, the locations where the previously listed elements of the business operate. (The fact that a business is distributed is often overlooked and can cause severe constraints and add unexpected complexity to the business and to the design and implementation of its systems. More on this when we discuss architecture in Chapter 4, "Architectural Modeling.")

"All in all, a business model shows the company's function in the world, what it does, how and when. The model should emphasize the architecture, that is, the static structures in the company, besides explaining the various flows of events, that is, the dynamic behavior of the elements in the architecture." [JACO1] These models need to show this information for the business as it exists today and as you want it to be tomorrow.

This sounds like quite an undertaking. To do everything in the prior two paragraphs would require a huge commitment of time and resources. This is why most companies do not attempt to develop a fully comprehensive model of their business. Business modeling is usually undertaken at a lesser scope within a division or sub-division or at a smaller, tactical level. In addition, it is almost always undertaken to achieve specific business goals or to eliminate noted weaknesses or acute problems. We will discuss this further in the upcoming section, "Should I Model My Entire Business?."

In this chapter, we will examine the UML models that will enable us to see and understand all the previously mentioned interacting elements of the business.

Why Should I Model My Business?

There are a number of reasons why you should model your business. These range from high-level business planning to the maintenance of operational IT systems. Let's examine just a few. Most businesses have a mission statement. If they don't, they at least have a company vision, whether it is written formally or not. How do you know if your company's systems are properly structured to deliver that vision? What do you do when the markets change, requiring your business to change? What systems need to change? How does that change impact the other systems in your enterprise?

Some business leaders take the "Blues Brothers" approach to achieving their mission. For those of you who haven't seen *The Blues Brothers* movie, here is a short summary. The Blues Brothers had a clear mission, but that was about all they had. They had only a half-baked plan, which drove them to improvise all along the way, depending on heroic intervention by many people to keep things on track throughout the process, wreaking havoc and destruction on the people and places they encountered, running afoul of the law, and landing in jail. They eventually achieved their mission, but at a very high cost. Great comedy, poor career choice.

You cannot effectively achieve your mission or change it without understanding where you are, where you want to go, and what you need to do to get there. Let's say that you want to develop a distinctive business competence, such as being the low-cost alternative, being the high-quality supplier, being the fastest competitor, or being the top service provider. Where would you look in your business to effect the changes that will bring you to that goal?

All these can be addressed with a good model of your business operations. Without that, you are simply relying on the memories of individual employees for all the detailed information required to build such a model. You really have a problem if some of those employees leave the company. Even if you have all the right people in the same room, you cannot effectively perform an analysis of your business and all the required changes in your collective heads. In addition, each person has a particular context and viewpoint, which are rarely articulated clearly enough for all the others to fully understand. A visual model is crucial for providing a common baseline from which you can move forward.

Now, you must use your judgment and not take this to the extreme either. You need to document this information in sufficient detail to ensure that everyone interprets it the correct way without going overboard.

From the Real World—Three Years in Three Days

I was working with a company on a task to assist the business people in building a three-year plan. The idea was to understand how they wanted to reorganize their division to meet changing customer needs, establish new business initiatives, and prepare a funding request to implement the changes. A team of a dozen or so people was assembled: vice presidents, division heads, senior staff, and a few senior IT people. Others were called in as needed. We met frequently, trying to hash out this three-year plan using a reputable structured methodology.

continues

From the Real World—Three Years in Three Days (*continued*)

We focused on the business planning stages of the methodology for the purpose of designing the new business structure and operation.

The meetings went on for weeks. The business people talked, the methodologist facilitated, the scribe captured volumes of information, and nothing was getting accomplished. One step forward, two steps back was the mode of operation. With deadlines looming, one of the team members pulled me aside and said, "You know that UML stuff. Do you think you can do anything with that to help here?"

So, I took the business VP and his two assistants into a room and started talking to them about their business. I did not try to teach them the UML, but as they were talking, I was at a flipchart, drawing *business use case diagrams* (more on these later in this chapter). Seeing these diagrams caused a flurry of detailed discussion about their business and about the other divisions, other businesses, government agencies, and customers it interacted with. We very quickly found the root cause of the lack of progress—these three senior business people, whose job was to run this division, did not agree on how their division operated.

This is a problem that we see far too often. These business folks were very smart and successful in running the division. However, nobody had the correct overall picture of how it all came together. Using use case diagrams, we completed the task in three days, whereas we had made little progress in the weeks we lost with the earlier approach.

Lessons Learned

1. You must understand your business as it exists today before making changes.

2. You must understand your business as you want it to be in the future so that you know where you are going.

3. No one person fully understands, nor can keep in his or her head, all the aspects of a business that is of significant size.

4. Do not overwhelm business people with technical terminology or tools. That's the job of the facilitator (modeler) to understand those things. Business folks run the business; modelers model.

5. A visual model of your business, even a very simple one, will provide the "point-of-focus" needed to discuss and resolve business issues.

Modeling is useful not only in planning future business operations, as in the previous example. We often have to deal with the existing systems that run our businesses as we develop new systems. The integration of "legacy" systems in our plans is a task we all must eventually deal with. However, these legacy systems are usually a mystery to all but a few remaining people in the company. Effectively addressing existing systems requires more than just knowing what services that system provides to your business. There is also the need to understand that existing system's details. The passing of this knowledge along to the people who inherit these systems is critical to the continuity of operations so that they can upgrade or maintain them. But how often is this done? Also, whatever system documentation exists is typically out of date. So, this knowledge transfer is usually done at the "physical" level, by passing the source code to the next programmer tasked to maintain the software. Eventually, the code may be understood in this manner, but the business function this system supports might be more obscure. Even in the best of situations, this is a costly and ineffective approach. Having a model of the existing system in a common, understandable language is a tremendous aid.

From the Real World—Tag! You're It!

When a senior programmer moves on to bigger and better things, it's always a challenge for her replacement to inherit, learn, and support their software. But what about when the user of that software moves on, too? This happened between system deliveries as part of a reorganization that occurred in my software development organization. I inherited a critical piece of software

- That had no documentation.
- Whose source code and data files were missing.
- Whose place in the overall business architecture was understood by only one person (the programmer who was leaving).
- Whose users did not understand the business or the technical concepts of how it was to operate.

I'm sure many of you have been there, too. How could this be a "critical" piece of software if it was left in this state? When it was written, it never was part of the official contract with their customer. It was built "off the books" (without documentation or configuration management) by a programmer who needed to solve a particular shortcoming of the system design.

continues

From the Real World—Tag! You're It! (*continued*)

Specifically, in this particular system, there was a possibility that the data being presented to the user was inaccurate. If this inaccurate data was acted upon, a catastrophic failure could result. This software detected those errors and reported them so these problems could be fixed prior to the subsystem going "live." This software saved thousands of hours of analysis that would have to have been done manually for every release of this system. (This situation happens often, particularly when dealing with software that is not part of daily operations, such as software that performs some form of testing, configuration, reporting, or initialization.)

I was the engineer that inherited this problem. Finding all the pieces of this software took weeks. Understanding its operation took a few more weeks. But really understanding the design and the original concepts behind its operation took months. For me personally, this was a great challenge. However, the organization could have used my time solving other problems. A model of not just the software but also of the enterprise architecture would have reduced this ramp up cost and time dramatically.

But that was only one level of the problem. The new users of this software didn't understand the concepts behind its use. So, what did they do? They constantly wrote defects (i.e., error reports) against this application that were not defects—that's the way the software was supposed to operate, but they did not understand. I spent a great deal of time constantly explaining to management, who kept seeing high numbers on defect reports, that these were not real defects. More lost time, more cost.

But this saga continues. We will return to this example in a later chapter.

Lessons Learned

1. Modeling your business and its legacy applications will help minimize the costs and impact on productivity when software is transitioned to new staff members.

2. A clear model of how your systems are to be used operationally will reduce the learning curve of new users. This will also help avoid unnecessary maintenance costs due to "pilot error" or misunderstanding.

> **3.** Configuration control of ALL software that performs key functions is imperative.
>
> **4.** When you are creating software for an external customer, put all software that you are responsible for providing in the contract.

Should I Model My Entire Business?

All too often, business or system development is tactical in nature. Although this may work in the short term, over time, you will end up with functions that do not interact well or multiple systems that are partially or fully redundant. They may serve their tactical purpose, but together they do not serve the needs of the business or the customer.

So theoretically and academically, you should model your entire business. Wouldn't it be great to have such a complete, comprehensive model prior to embarking on any development project? However, in practice, this is one of the most difficult things to accomplish, for reasons both technical and political. Nonetheless, there are situations where taking on this challenge is worth the effort, such as the following:

- If you have an overarching objective that will transform most or all of your business
- If you have a project or set of interrelated projects that will take years to implement
- If you are adding a unique or unprecedented business function
- If you are changing part of your business that has many complex relationships with other parts of your business or with external businesses

In other words, if what you are planning is big, complex, ground-breaking, or long-lived, a full business model is worth the investment. The benefits are many:

- You develop a correct and common understanding of your business (making this knowledge explicit is critical to avoiding costly missteps).
- You can manage complexity more effectively (remember that complexity increases geometrically as the number of interrelationships between business functions [or systems] increases).

- You know your starting point for change. (Have you ever used an online map service to ask for directions to a destination? Does it work if you don't tell it where your are starting from?)
- You have a stable foundation for managing large or multiple projects (now you have the map and you can tell where you are on your journey).
- You can establish ownership and funding responsibilities. (Who is responsible for this part of the business and what business unit is paying for the changes?)

From the Real World—Sssssshhhhh. Don't Move.

I was working on a project that was intended to bring a new and valuable service to customers, that was leading-edge in the marketplace, and that affected multiple divisions of the business. I was assigned to the project near the end of the design phase. Unlike many development projects, the business people were involved regularly in this project—partly because it affected their divisions, but mostly because it was a high-profile project. A successful project would translate into direct success in their careers.

At the end of design, the consulting firm that was going to perform the implementation presented us with the expected cost to finish the project—$1.2 million. The project had already cost $0.75 million. This was big money at this mid-sized company. A meeting was held to discuss whether to go forward. In discussing the cost, one brave soul asked the critical question, "Who owns this project?" Silence. Not a single VP or department head moved a muscle, as if a hooded cobra had just been dropped on the table. The prolonged silence was finally broken by that brave soul who pressed the question. Immediately, a verbal tennis match broke out with each department making the case that the project belonged to another department.

Understand that there were also technical reasons not to proceed to implementation yet. But those weren't enough to delay implementation—after all, careers would be made on this project. But when the ownership and funding issues became explicit, it was not long before the project was cancelled.

Lessons Learned

1. A model of your business and the planned changes will make owner-ship and responsibility issues clear, before it's too late.
2. Technical professionals must understand that non-technical issues may be more powerful deciding factors than technical issues (e.g., politics, ego, and careers).

How Can the UML Help Me Improve My Business?

When you have a model of your existing business, you can ensure that all stakeholders understand the current business. However, this requires a model that can be understood by all parties. Using UML as the common language enables this understanding. With a concise UML model, you can find potential areas for change, such as the following:

- Inefficiencies
- Performance issues
- Redundant processes
- Incorrect or conflicting business rules
- Exposures (i.e., areas of risk to your business or systems)
- Potential areas for consolidation, efficiencies, or other improvements
- Underutilized or overutilized systems or people

The last point here highlights one fact often forgotten when designing busi-nesses and systems—there are *people* in your business. You model not only the things in the business but also the people and what they do, too.

How Do I Model My Business Using the UML?

When modeling your business using the UML, it's a good idea to start by considering three interrelated questions:

- Who do you do business with?
- What do they want your business to do for them, or vice versa?
- How does your business meet its needs?

These three simple questions set the context in which your business operates. As an example, let us say you are running a retail business. Who are you doing business with? Who are the people, companies, or systems that come to do business with you? For a retail store, this could include the traditional customers, shipping companies, suppliers, credit-card companies, and so forth. All these people, businesses, and systems play a *role* in dealing with your business. They are called *business actors* (they play a *role*, as real-world actors do; see Figure 2-3).

Retail Customer   **Salesperson**   **Credit Company**

Figure 2-3 *UML business actors for a retail system.*

Why do these business actors come to you? For what reasons do they interact with your business? In retail, the business actors may want to do the following:

- Purchase products
- Return products
- Deliver products to customers
- Deliver products to your stores
- Bill customers
- And more

Now that you know what the business actors want, how will your business meet their needs? What services or business functions do you provide to meet those needs? Some typical business functions in retail might be the following:

- Retail sales
- Billing
- Inventory management
- Shipping

These are the individual *cases* of how the business actors will *use* your *business*. In the Rational Unified Process [RUP1], these are referred to as *business use cases* (see Figure 2-4).

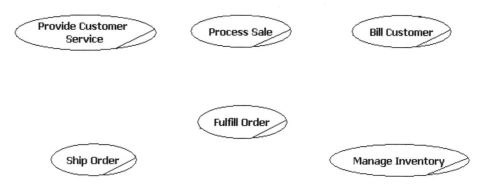

Figure 2-4   *UML business use cases for a retail system.*

Business Use Case Model

Bringing these elements (business actors and business use cases) together, we create the *business use case model* for your business.

Business Use Case Diagrams

We start with a *business use case diagram,* which provides the *context* in which your business operates. It depicts what is outside of your business (the business actors), what is inside the business (the business use cases), and the relationships between the two (see Figure 2-5). "A business use case diagram is a diagram of the intended functions of the business and is used as an

essential input to identify roles and deliverables in the organization." [LEFF1]
It is a *context diagram* for your business.

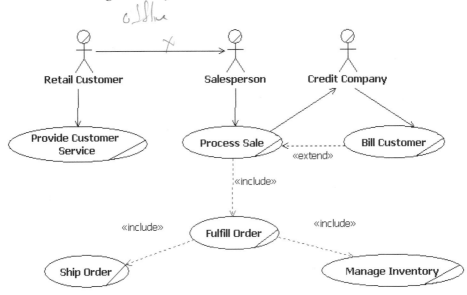

Figure 2-5 *Business use case diagram.*

The lines with arrowheads in business use case diagrams are *associations*
between the business actor and the business use case. They indicate a relationship between the two model elements they connect. The direction of the
arrow shows which element initiates the activity. In the example in Figure
2-5, the salesperson uses (i.e., initiates) the Process Sale business use case. An
association can exist without an arrowhead. This represents a bi-directional
communication path. (The <<include>> and <<extend>> notation will be
discussed in Chapter 3, along with more about use cases in general.)

From the Real World—That's Not Right! I'm Calling the UML Police!

We told you that we would be pragmatic in this book. The preceding
discussion qualifies. Technically, having an arrowhead on the associations
between actors and use cases is not permitted. However, when designing
systems in the real world, this minor deviation has value. In moderate-sized
systems that may have, for example, six use cases, you could easily have
over a dozen actors. In large systems or in enterprise-level design (systems

of systems), there can be many more. Using arrows enables you to immediately see which actors are active (initiating use cases) and which are passive (instead of initiating a use case, the use case may be providing something to that actor).

Having an association between actors is also not allowed, but in the real world, actors do communicate directly with each other, particularly if they are people. This is important to depict so that you correctly represent how your business operates. Seeing the arrows between actors may cause you to decide that such an interaction should not occur, or maybe it should be automated—an important decision for your business and your system architecture.

Now we do not recommend that you redefine the UML's semantics for every fleeting whim. (We have seen projects try that—and fail miserably.) Just keep in mind that a key purpose for using the UML is communication. That's what it's all about—getting your ideas across to others. Sometimes, small tweaks can add big value, even if they are not "by the book."

Lessons Learned

1. The goal of using the UML is to clearly express your designs, not to conform blindly to the UML specification.
2. If being "creative" in your use of the UML achieves this goal, that's fine. Just be careful not to completely redefine the UML semantics or use its elements in ways that could be interpreted incorrectly by others. In other words, be very careful.

Now that you have established the business use cases, you need to define what they mean. Never assume that everyone knows or agrees on what these major business functions are or what they do. (Remember the "Real World—Three Years in Three Days" example earlier.) To make this knowledge explicit, you should write a short description of each business use case's function. The description should provide an overview: what the business use case is, what it does and why (i.e., its "mission"), when it is used, and any other important information specific to this business use case. This should be one or two paragraphs, just enough so that anyone could read that definition and understand the overall purpose of the business use case. For example, if the business use case is "account management," the description might read:

> **Account management:** This business use case provides services that enable the small business and retail customers, at a branch office, during normal business hours, to perform actions regarding savings and checking accounts. These would include opening, closing, transferring, changing registration of, and merging accounts. This use case does not include account inquiries, deposits, withdrawals, or online functions.

Once agreed to, this provides the context for developing the details of the business use case. This is done using *activity diagrams*.

Activity Diagrams

Now that you know the people, businesses, and systems you interact with and what services you provide to meet their needs, you need to understand *how* they interact to provide that service. What are the details behind each of the business use cases? For example, for the Process Sale business use case, how does a customer actually purchase a retail product? What are the steps taken and by whom? That transaction could take place like this:

1. Customer enters store and chooses product(s).
2. Customer presents product to salesperson.
3. Salesperson scans product (repeat for all products).
4. Salesperson provides total cost.
5. Salesperson inquires as to payment method.
6. Customer provides payment.
7. Payment is accepted by salesperson.
8. Receipt and product are given to customer.

Or it could be:

1. Customer enters store and chooses product(s).
2. Customer presents product to salesperson.
3. Salesperson inquires as to payment method.

4. If payment by credit card, customer provides card to salesperson (if not, go to step 6).

5. Salesperson swipes card.

6. Salesperson scans product (repeat for all products).

7. Salesperson provides total cost.

8. If payment by credit card, customer authorizes payment. (Otherwise, customer provides payment and payment is accepted by salesperson.)

9. Receipt and product are given to customer.

Or even:

1. Customer enters store and chooses product(s).

2. Customer inserts credit or debit card into scanning station.

3. Customer scans product (repeat for all products).

4. Scanning station provides total cost.

5. Customer authorizes payment.

6. Payment is validated.

7. Receipt is given to customer.

Although this sounds like a simple process flow, as you can see, there could be many different ways this transaction might take place. That is why it is critical to get agreement on the workflow. Real workflows are more complex than this example, with many decision points, alternate paths, and combinations of activities. That is why a visual model is important. An activity diagram can depict such flows in a way that is easy to follow and understand.

Let's revisit the first variant of this transaction, as described previously, using an activity diagram. Activity diagrams show the interactions between the business actors and your business. Let's begin at the beginning:

1. Customer enters store and chooses product(s).

2. Customer presents product to salesperson.

3. Salesperson scans product (repeat for all products).

This gives us the beginnings of the activity diagram for the Process Sale business use case (see Figure 2-6).

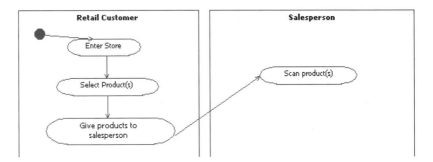

Figure 2-6   *Retail sale activity diagram, steps 1–3.*

Here, you see that the two business actors' names (Retail Customer, Salesperson) are shown at the top of the columns in the diagram. These columns are called *swimlanes*. (Note that in UML 2.0, these are referred to as *partitions*.) Any *activity* (shown in the ovals—note that in UML 2.0, these are called "actions." UML 2.0 still has an element called an activity, which can contain actions and control nodes and is used to specify behavior) in a given column is performed by the person, organization, or system listed at the top of the swimlane. The flow starts at the *start state* (the solid dot) and flows as indicated by the arrows.

Even at this early point, the activity diagram shows an area that needs to be discussed by your team. This flow says the salesperson scans the product. Who said there is a scanner? A scanner is an implementation decision that you seem to be making very early in the development of your system. Generally, this is not a wise thing to do. There are still some stores out there that do not have UPC scanners. They still enter the prices by hand. These diagrams can help you challenge your assumptions early, before costly implementation begins.

In fact, if the scanner fails, the salesperson would need to enter the price by hand (or maybe even have to perform the dreaded "price check"). Here is the first case of finding an *alternate flow*. When doing your initial activity diagrams, it is a good approach to diagram the best-case scenario first and then go back later and add the alternate scenarios that you discover.

Continuing:

4. Salesperson provides total cost.
5. Salesperson inquires as to payment method.

See Figure 2-7.

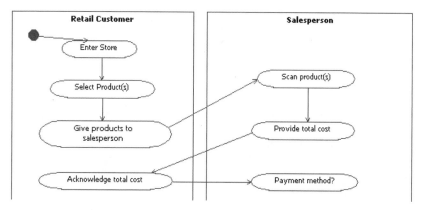

Figure 2-7 *Retail sale activity diagram, steps 4–5.*

Hold on! What is this "customer acknowledgment" activity? That is not in the original flow. As we created this diagram, we realized that having the work-flow go directly from step 4 to step 5 was not really correct. If it was correct, why would the salesperson provide the total cost to the customer if the customer just immediately moves to asking about the payment? The reason the salesperson provides the total cost is to give the customer an opportunity to object. What if the customer does not have enough money to pay for everything? What if the price from the scanner is different from what the customer read on the price tag? Here, we see the value of these diagrams in providing the opportunity to question the business workflow (which looked fine in text format but was shown to be wrong when diagrammed) and raising the possibilities of additional alternate workflows. Continuing with the workflow:

6. Customer provides payment.
7. Payment is accepted by salesperson.

See Figure 2-8.

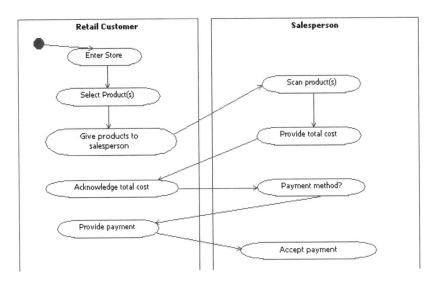

Figure 2-8   *Retail sale activity diagram, steps 6–7.*

Here, we add the payment. We can see this is obviously too simple. This flow should vary based on payment method (cash, credit, gift certificate, coupons, discount card, etc.). This is another set of alternate flows to revisit later. Continuing with the workflow:

8. Receipt and product are given to customer.

See Figure 2-9.

Which is given to the customer first…the receipt or the product purchased? In this case, it does not matter. These activities can happen in parallel. This is shown in the activity diagram by using a *synchronization point* (the horizontal black bar). The two flows that come *out* of the bar indicate they can happen independently. When two (or more) flows come *into* a synchronization point, this indicates that the workflow cannot continue until all the inflowing activities are complete.

We have also added a *terminating activity*, Customer Leaves, to the flow. At first glance, this does not seem to add much value, but it does add clarity so that you can see explicitly how this interaction between your business actor and your business use case ends. Also, if this were to be an online store, Customer Leaves would have many business and application design implications. For instance, when your customer leaves your online store (i.e., your web site), you could not immediately give the products to the customer—instead, the business flow would initiate a fulfillment activity, and that in turn would cause you to modify the payment activities because you would need to account for shipping and handling charges. You could not give the customer a receipt—but you could send them an email receipt. The explicit end of the flow is shown at the *end state* (bull's-eye) symbol.

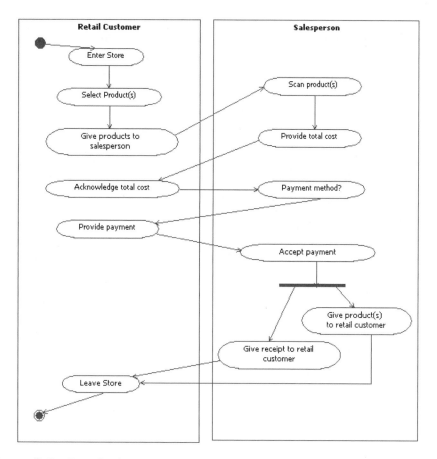

Figure 2-9   *Retail sale activity diagram, step 8.*

The end of this workflow might raise the question, "Why not have 'Give Receipt to Retail Customer' and 'Give Product to Retail Customer' both flow into a synchronization point to ensure that the customer does not leave without her product or receipt?" This is a good question that you should consider. The answer depends on how you want to have your business operate. Are you going to take any overt actions to ensure that the customer can't leave without both her products and receipts (some stores *do* check your receipts as you leave)? If so, the additional sync point is a good idea. If your business is going to take no such actions, it would be incorrect to add the sync point. These are the kinds of issues that rarely come out with purely textual specifications. Visual models make things and their relationships obvious and thus provide the level of focus that simple text cannot.

Alternate Flows

Developing that simple activity diagram raised a number of questions that need to be resolved for the workflow of the Process Sale business use case. Many of them were possible alternate flows:

- Scanner fails, manual price entry.
- Scanner fails, price information not available to salesperson, manual price check.
- Customer does not accept total price, insufficient funds, cancel entire sale.
- Customer does not accept total price, insufficient funds, exclude one or more products from sale.
- Customer does not accept total price, expecting different price, resolve pricing.
- Customer does not accept total price, doesn't want to pay that much, cancel sale.
- Payment method is rejected (e.g., store only accepts certain credit cards).

...and so forth.

These flows can be depicted using a *decision point* (shown as a diamond). You can see how these can be used in the alternate flow for scanner problems in Figure 2-10.

In summary, business use case diagrams provide a context for your business—what is inside the business and what is outside. They show which people or systems interact with your business. They capture the interfaces between your business and the world outside. Activity diagrams depict the basic workflow of how a business operates. They define in more detail the *interface* between your business and the business actors. They enable you to understand how people or systems interact with your business, the processes that are followed, and the activities that are performed. In this way, you obtain a basic understanding of the way the job gets done.

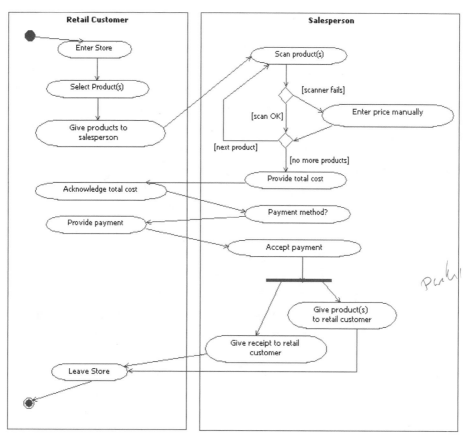

Figure 2-10 *Retail sale activity diagram, decision point.*

Watch Out—Business Rules

Business rules are policies, constraints, or other rules that you impose on your business. For example, "a savings account can have as many as two owners" is a business rule. As you start to develop your activity diagrams, you are starting to create, implicitly or explicitly, business rules. You will see them start to take shape here and in subsequent diagrams. They will be further developed in the upcoming *sequence diagrams* and eventually take form in the design of the system, when you reach the *class diagrams*. The caveat here is to be aware that you are creating such rules and to do so consciously.

From the Real World—The "25 Rule"

The rental-car shuttle bus was waiting to leave to return us to the airport. In typical fashion, the driver came around and asked everyone to which airline they were going. The young man sitting next to me fumbled over his words for a moment, then sheepishly looked up at the driver. He said he wasn't going to the airport. He needed to go to another rental car company. This was puzzling but became more so when the driver said, "Ah. The 25 rule, eh?" The young man nodded.

This riveted my attention. I had to ask about this "25 rule." I found that in most areas of the United States, you can't rent a car from many rental car companies unless you are over 25 years of age. This young man had a reservation for a rental car, but when he arrived at the lot, the rental people there invoked the "25 rule."

This major rental car company had obviously never modeled the business. Otherwise, why would their reservation people give the gentleman a reservation, only to have the fulfillment people at the rental site deny him a car? This lack of an integrated business (i.e., Reservations and Rental Fulfillment not operating by the same business rules) costs the company time and money, misuses personnel and equipment, incurs an opportunity cost, and definitely does not please the customer.

Lessons Learned

1. Modeling your business makes clear how different part of your business interact.
2. Modeling your business makes your business rules explicit.

Business Analysis Model

Now that you have established what you do for those business actors outside your business, you need to ask:

- What is my business going to do internally to provide the services the business actors want?

- What people, assets, information, etc. will we use to provide such services?

So, let's say you have completed the business use case models for the Process Sale, Bill Customer, Manage Inventory, and Ship Order business use cases of your retail store. You look at the business use case diagrams and activity diagrams, and you determine that there are a number of internal people in your business that are involved in these activities. These *business workers* are shown in Figure 2-11.

Figure 2-11   *UML business workers.*

These workers have to use assets of your business to accomplish their functions. Some of these assets, or *business entities*, for the retail system are shown in Figure 2-12.

Figure 2-12   *UML business entities.*

How do these business workers and entities relate? That is depicted in the *business analysis model*. This is an inside look at how your people (the business workers) interact with other business workers, business actors, and business entities to achieve the business processes (i.e., business use cases) that were just defined in the business use case model.

Look to the business use case model and activity diagrams to give you the starting information you need to create the business analysis model. You then add how you desire your business to operate internally, that is, the design of your in-house business operation. In this case, from the prior models, we know customers will be buying products (we hope). Product would be a business entity. Thus, we derive that we must maintain an inventory (also a business entity) of products. Therefore, we need an inventory worker to maintain the inventory of our products. Let's say that our business use case model has also specified that customers may order a group of products, which they want to be shipped to them. Therefore, we determine the need for a shipping worker (business worker) to create a shipping schedule (business entity) and an inventory worker (business worker) to assemble the order (business entity).

A partial *business objects diagram* for these requirements is shown in Figure 2-13. Technically, this is a class diagram (more on these in Chapter 4). However, because the typical class diagram you will see looks very different (they use different icons), to avoid confusion, we distinguish the two by calling these business objects diagrams. We use this name because this diagram depicts the things (i.e., the objects) that are used in your business to perform its function.

As part of the business analysis model, the business objects diagram shows the static relationships between the people and things in your system. In Figure 2-13, you see a new type of association—an *aggregation* (shown as a line with a hollow diamond on one end). An aggregation indicates that one thing is part of another. In this figure, a product is part of an order. But what does that really mean?

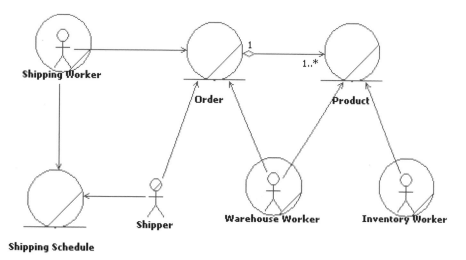

Figure 2-13 *Business objects diagram (partial) for retail system.*

Watch Out—What ARE You Modeling?

You have to be careful that you make clear the aspect of the things you are modeling. In the preceding example, we said that a product is part of an order. As we have modeled this in Figure 2-13, we are not modeling the actual physical products and the physical "order" that arrives on your doorstep. We are modeling the informational aspects of the products that are in the order. This would manifest itself in the real world as a packing list, for example. How do we show this? Through the use of an aggregation. Another way to think of such a relationship is the idea of *containment*—not physical, but a logical containment, as might be represented in a bill of materials or a parts list. If you want to represent a more physical containment, this would be shown with a composition aggregation. (This is depicted similarly to an aggregation, but the diamond on the association is solid.) What's the difference? With composition, the product may only exist in one order (i.e., you and I cannot both receive the same physical product). With aggregation, both of our packing lists can have the same product on them. We will discuss aggregation and composition further in Chapter 5.

To be more explicit, you can add numbers to the ends of associations to indicate how many things participate in the relationship. This is called *multiplicity*. In this case, there is a "1..*" annotation on the order-product association on the product end. This means an order can contain "one or many" products (the asterisk means "many"). The other end of the association shows a "1," which indicates that a product may be part of only one order. Multiplicity can be shown as a single number (e.g., 5) or as a range (e.g., 0–12, meaning between 0 and 12 things can participate in the association, or 7-*, meaning from seven to an unlimited number of participants). Multiplicity will be discussed further in Chapters 4 and 5.

Sequence Diagrams

The previous business objects diagram captured the static relationships between the things in your business. You now need to establish the dynamic interaction of these things in operation over time. This can be depicted in a type of UML *interaction diagram* called a *sequence diagram*. A sequence diagram shows all the interactions between the model elements for a given scenario in time order. (Sequence diagram basics, discussed here, have been augmented in UML 2.0. These changes will be discussed in Chapter 8, "Is That All There Is?.")

Using the information from the previous models, we show how a sale would be processed for a telephone order of some products (again starting with a best case scenario). First, the customer initiates a call to your telesalesperson, and basic information is gathered (see Figure 2-14).

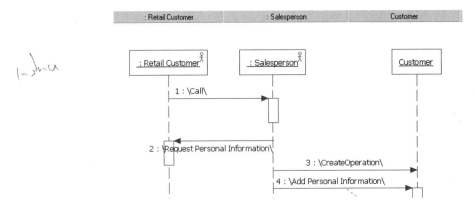

Figure 2-14   *Sequence diagram for retail sale (initial).*

Reading down the diagram vertically (time flows downward), we see that the customer calls our salesperson, who needs to gather information on the customer. (The arrows on this diagram indicate the interactions that flow between the various model elements. The lines that run vertically below the model elements are called *lifelines*.) Thus, we need to create a new business entity, Customer. (This obviously is not the same as the business actor customer. The business actor is external to the system. The business entity Customer resides inside our system and is a *proxy*, that is, a substitute or surrogate that represents the real customer. This will likely manifest itself during implementation as a record in a customer database.) The salesperson asks the Customer for his or her personal information and adds it to the customer business entity. You can see how this process of incrementally performing more detailed modeling results in the discovery of additional key elements of our system.

The customer then orders various products (see Figure 2-15). This requires the salesperson to create an order and add products to the order. This is repeated for all products. The order is completed, the price is calculated, and the total price is provided to the customer. You will note the *recursive* message, "Calculate Total Price," that flows out of and then back to the order's lifeline. This merely indicates that order knows that it needs to calculate its own price and does so. This may seem an odd situation—an order calculating its own price? But in object-oriented systems, this is quite common. Responsibilities are typically assigned to the element (or object) that holds the information necessary to fulfill them. In this way, the information can remain encapsulated in one element.

Then, the customer provides credit-card information to the salesperson, who stores that information in the customer business entity and also sends it and the total price of the order to the credit-card company (a new business actor not previously identified) for verification (see Figure 2-16). Note how key information, such as name, credit-card number, expiration date, and total price, are passed as parameters of the message "verify credit information." This is needed to determine if the customer has sufficient credit. The credit-card company approves, and the order number is given to the customer.

You can see how further development of the business models drives out critical details that may have been overlooked in the initial pass. In fact, this type of modeling is quite iterative.

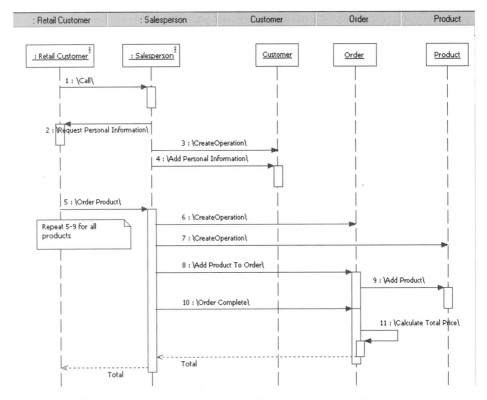

Figure 2-15 *Sequence diagram for retail sale (creating order).*

From the Real World—Doesn't Play Well with Other Children

We were working with a customer on using the UML for database design. On our last day, I was leaving for our final meeting when I saw that my rental car and three others had been broken into (eight o'clock in the morning, right in front of the hotel), and all the contents had been stolen—luggage, laptop, everything was gone. All I had was my cell phone. I called the police. They came, did the interviews, and kept the car to dust for fingerprints, etc. After the meeting, we went to the airport. After finishing all the exciting paperwork about the theft with the rental car company, we flew home.

A few days later, I realized I never paid the rental car company for the days I used the car. I called customer service and explained the situation, and the very courteous service agent was glad to help me. Then she asked, "May I have your rental agreement number?" I had just told her everything was stolen. I didn't have the rental agreement number or even the rental agreement. That was OK. She offered a solution. She said I should go to the rental desk at the airport where I picked up the car. They might still have the rental paperwork around. I should get the rental agreement number from them and call her back. Then I could give the number to her, and she would be able to help me give her the payment. I should fly back to Atlanta to get the number and call her back? Not likely!

We can see here that, although the individual systems the rental car company had in place (reservations, rental, customer service systems) did their individual jobs, they did not work in concert to serve the businesses needs (i.e., to get paid). The individual systems did not share one of the most important pieces of data their own business created—the rental agreement number. Obviously, the company never modeled any use case (if any at all) where the customer may not have a rental agreement number (e.g., car stolen, rental agreement lost, billing error, etc.)—a parameter that would be easily shown in a sequence diagram as being passed across business functions. Therefore, their systems could not interoperate effectively.

Lessons Learned

1. Along with the physical aspects (e.g., people, things) of your business, model the operation of the business, too.

2. Create models of your business systems to understand how they will operate together.

3. Remember to consider how your various systems interact to provide your business services.

4. Leave nothing in your car unattended.

You can also see where these models position you to easily refine your business processes further. Consider the sequence diagram in Figure 2-15. Prudence would dictate that before adding a product to the order, you check inventory to see if it is in stock. This is easily done by adding the Inventory business entity and the appropriate messages to and from it. Another consideration—the storing of the credit-card information in Customer. Although this seems like a reasonable thing to do, you should consider it carefully.

Doing so implies that you need to create processes to update, delete, and report on that information. Or do you just plan to keep repeatedly dumping information into Customer on every purchase?

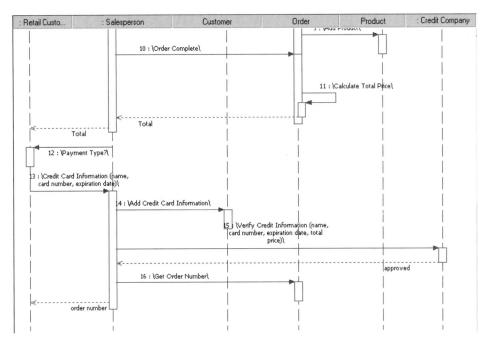

Figure 2-16 *Sequence diagram for retail sale (payment processing).*

In summary, a business analysis model establishes what you do inside your business to fulfill its purpose. The business objects model shows which people use which things to complete their function. Sequence diagrams show how these elements interact with each other to complete the various business scenarios. Together these provide the internal view of how your business responds to requests from the outside world.

Taken together, the business use case model and the business analysis model depict how "business can be described in terms of processes that achieve goals by collaborating with different types of resource objects." [ERIK1]

Topics to Consider

You may want to examine these additional topics:

- Collaboration diagrams—Another type of interaction diagram (like sequence diagrams) where the model elements are the center of focus instead of focusing on the message flows (as in sequence diagrams).
- Generalization association—An association that indicates that one thing is a "type of" another thing (e.g., a truck is a type of vehicle). How might this be used with business actors?
- How might each of your business model diagrams be affected if a corporate business goal was for your business to be the low-cost supplier versus being the top service provider?
- You can find many of the concepts in this chapter (e.g., business use case model, business analysis model) further elaborated upon in the Rational Unified Process. [RUP2]

Terms

Business use case	Business use case model
Business analysis model	Activity diagram
Sequence diagram	Use case diagram
Business actor	Business objects diagram
Context diagram	Association
Activity	Swimlane
Start state	End state
Aggregation	Containment
Decision point	Interface
Class diagram	Business worker
Multiplicity	Interaction diagram
Message	Lifeline
Proxy	Collaboration diagram
Generalization	Partition
Synchronization point	Role

Summary

This chapter started with a discussion of business model. You learned the importance of modeling your current and future business and ways that modeling can help you improve your business. You saw examples where modeling would help not only in system development but also in project management (planning and funding) and even in software maintenance.

We then examined how to go about modeling your business with UML. You learned how the business use case model establishes what is inside and outside your business using a business use case diagram and the workflows using activity diagrams. You saw numerous UML elements used in business modeling: business actors, business use cases, associations, activities, synchronization points, decision points, and swimlanes. We also examined how establishing alternate flows cannot only capture workflow variants but also can reveal limitations and enhancements to the existing workflows.

We then moved to the business analysis model. Here the business objects diagram was used to establish the relationships between your business assets that are used to accomplish the business use cases. This was followed by an examination of sequence diagrams to show the dynamic interaction of these business assets. You learned about business workers, business entities, aggregation, multiplicity, and lifelines.

Review Questions

1. When is it recommended to not model the business as it currently exists and to model the business only as you want it to be in the future?

2. Name two situations where you should model your entire business.

3. What is the purpose of the business analysis model?

4. True or False: Activity diagrams show the time-ordered sequence of message flows between the elements in your model.

5. The business use case diagram:

   a. Shows the business workflow

   b. Shows the configuration of your business's hardware

   c. Shows how your business internally satisfies your customers' requests

   d. Shows the context of your business

6. Name three areas where business modeling can improve your business.

[ERIK1] Eriksson, Hans-Erik and Magnus Penker. 2000. *Business Modeling with UML: Business Patterns at Work*. John Wiley & Sons, Inc.

[JACO1] Jacobson, Ivar, Maria Ericsson, and Agneta Jacobson. 1995. *The Object Advantage: Business Process Reengineering with Object Technology*. Addison-Wesley.

[LEFF1] Leffingwell, Dean and Don Widrig. 2000. *Managing Software Requirements: A Unified Approach*. Boston: Addison-Wesley.

[RUP1] [RUP2] Rational Unified Process, 1987–2003, IBM.

3

Requirements Modeling

Topics Covered in This Chapter

What Are Requirements?

Why Bother with Requirements?

What Types of Requirements Are There?

How Can the UML Model Requirements?

>   Review of Use Case Basics

>   More on Use Cases

>   Review of Sequence Diagram Basics

>   More on Sequence Diagrams

Topics to Consider

Terms

Summary

Review Questions

What Are Requirements?

Depending on the type of restaurants you frequent, your dining experience may differ significantly. At the first type of restaurant, you might drive up to the menu board. While reading the menu, a distorted voice comes through a cheap speaker and says something that is completely unintelligible. You respond by ordering what you want. The voice says something else you cannot understand. You drive around to the pickup window, pay for and receive your meal in a bag, and leave.

At a different establishment, a waiter comes to your table and greets you, asks about any immediate needs you have (adult beverages, soft drinks, water, etc.), provides you with menus, and leaves you to contemplate your choices. (The amount of time you get to review the menu always seems to be inversely proportional to the size of the menu.) The waiter returns and proceeds to tell you about any special meals that are available. When he completes his recitation, you place your order. Depending on the type of restaurant, your scenario varies.

The orders you place at restaurants are your *requirements* for your meal. They are the essential specifications, details, and terms of the contract, in this case, between you and the restaurant. The restaurant attempts to satisfy these requirements (thus meeting your needs, in this case, satisfying your specific hunger), though with varying levels of success. The better you define what you want (the requirements), the more satisfied you generally are with what is delivered to you.

One common definition of a requirement is "a software capability needed by the user to solve a problem that will achieve an objective." [DORF1]

From the Real World—Tag! You're It! (Reprise)

In the real world, not all demands for software and other capabilities will meet such an exacting definition. Remember from the last chapter the orphaned software I inherited from a programmer who had moved on? You will recall the users wrote numerous incorrect defects because they did not understand what the software was required to do. One of those users kept hounding management to have the software changed so that it didn't report so many errors. However, reporting errors was the primary function of the application! This change he asked for was not "a software capability needed by the user"—it was not *needed* at all. It was something he *wanted*. (Hence, I refer to these as *desirements*, not requirements.) This change would not "solve a problem"—indeed, this change would cause problems. However, the change would "achieve an objective"—this fellow simply did not want to have to check out all the reported errors; he didn't have the time.

Lessons Learned

1. Be aware that in the real world, a "requirement" may merely be something that someone wants.

2. You may have to satisfy desirements and requirements. (I was eventually directed to engineer a solution to satisfy this fellow's desirement without compromising the correctness of the application—a great deal of work for very little value.)

The sidebar is an example of why we prefer the following definition of requirements:

> "A requirement is an expression of a perceived need that something be accomplished or realized. Note that this definition is intended to encompass all defined requirements for a project. In particular, it includes the following:
>
> - Product, work, programmatic, service, and other requirements (including those commonly called 'constraints')
> - Incorrect requirements, i.e. requirements which are not valid statements of the customer's needs, although they may be perceived as such
> - Poor requirements and poorly expressed requirements
> - The expression of needs in different forms, not necessarily statements in natural language
> - Requirements expressed in technical and non-technical language
> - Wants and desires, noting that these are normally expressed as needs
> - Requirements which may not be binding or which are prioritized" [GABB1]

This much broader definition takes into account the real-world truth about "requirements" that we all need to be prepared to encounter.

Why Bother with Requirements?

Numerous studies have shown that some of the top reasons for the high rate of project failure result directly from requirements problems. Lack of requirements, misunderstood requirements, vague requirements, incomplete requirements, and changing requirements all are major failure points in system development. Such failures waste precious money, resources, and time. You have to know where you are going, or you'll never get there. That is the purpose of requirements.

Sometimes, I hear developers say they don't want to be saddled down with requirements. When asked "Why?" they often respond that they want or need to get started coding. But what will you code? That's like a builder saying he has to hurry up and lay brick, without really knowing where the property lines are, the orientation of the house, its size, where the utilities are, how many chimneys to build, or even if the homebuyer wants a brick house.

Also, rework is costly in construction of homes or in construction of software. The cost rises as time passes [LEFF2] (see Figure 3-1).

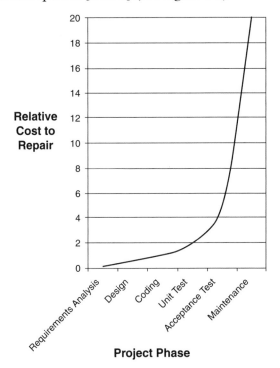

Figure 3-1   *Cost to repair defects over time.*

Also, without requirements, how do you know when you are *done*? Without the requirements to specify what needs to be built, the customer can keep telling you to change this or that ad nauseam (also known as *scope creep*). Having agreed-to requirements sets your goal, and you can execute tests against them to prove to the customer that you have reached that goal. Without requirements, you may never be "done" until the customer says so. If your original excuse for not having requirements was to get started coding sooner, wouldn't you also want to be done sooner? In addition, if you are working under contract that doesn't clearly define what you are to deliver, you might wait a long time for your payment.

Well-documented requirements will enable you to validate that your team is building what the customer expected. With the many regulations that exist throughout different industries today, such as BASEL II, Sarbanes Oxley, 21 CFR Part 11 [BASE1], and others, it's more important than ever to be able to prove that you are building what you said you would.

Requirements comprise the contract between you and your stakeholders that specifies what the system you are going to build will do to support their vision of the business (as expressed in the business models). In the end, you do not want to hear that what you built is not what they wanted. That scenario can cost you too much time, money, and maybe even your job or your business.

What Types of Requirements Are There?

Requirements come in many types: size, weight, operation, safety, regulatory, and so forth. However, they can be put into two higher-level categories— functional requirements and nonfunctional requirement. Functional requirements are those that relate to the "functioning" of the system. For example, "The system shall display the company name, ticker symbol, current share price, and percentage change from yesterday's closing price on one line." Functional requirements are the things that the system must "do."

Nonfunctional requirements relate to the characteristics of the system as a whole: reliability, scalability, performance, mean time between failure, etc. For example, "The system shall operate at a 99.99% reliability 24 hours per day." Nonfunctional requirements are the way the system as a whole must "be."

How Can the UML Model Requirements?

The concept of modeling requirements often strikes people as odd. Most of us think of requirements in the form that we usually see them—the written word. So, how do you model words?

Well, you don't. Think of "modeling" requirements as an exercise in organization. Most systems have dozens, hundreds, or in large systems, thousands of requirements. The only way to mentally grasp these requirements is to organize them into understandable chunks. You can do this organization in many ways—by function, location, platform, management structure (not a good choice), performance needs, and so on. However, many of these choices would begin to constrain the future designs before you even fully understand the needs of the users. In other words, it's too early to interject such restrictions (but you may do so later in the development lifecycle). So, how should you begin?

Review of Use Case Basics

At this point, if you have done your business modeling (as discussed previously), you know much about your customer and how she wants to run her business (or at least how she runs it today). This is what makes *use cases* a great way to begin your requirements modeling. Use cases organize your system by describing how the system is used. Not only does this leverage all the work you have done while business modeling, but this approach also serves as a bridge between what the business wants to be (which is expressed in the business models) and what your system design will be (which is expressed in your future architecture and application design models). This approach also keeps you focused on the customer, which is often forgotten in systems development.

As the earlier discussion on business modeling showed, a business use case depicts how the business actors will use your business and the intended functions of the business. However, remember that those were *business* use cases. They are much larger and broader in scope than the system-level use cases we will be talking about here.

More on Use Cases

Taken together, the *system use cases* provide the functionality specified by the business use cases. These system use cases will capture the scenarios of how the various actors will use the system you are building. For example, if your business is all about handheld Global Positioning System (GPS) devices, one of your business use cases might be Provide Positioning Services, whereas an application-level use case in this same domain might be Report Location.

Watch Out—"This Is Easy"

Do not be lulled by the apparent simplicity of use cases. They are *not* just blobs of functionality. Most people who read about creating use cases, will read the first few defining sentences and then mentally drift away. Although the concepts are simple, the use and the semantics of use cases are important. Most people starting out with UML gloss over these facts, and then use cases become difficult for them to develop correctly. This inevitably leads to problems later in development. You must understand some key characteristics of use cases in order to successfully use them.

Key Characteristics of Use Cases

Let us examine the vital characteristics of use cases and the related pitfalls by way of analogy—a map. Use cases specify the behavior of a system as individual, complete scenarios. A map specifies how to reach a destination by depicting a complete route. Use cases do not specify only part of a scenario, only individual steps in a scenario, or individual functions of your application. Similarly, a map would not be useful if it only showed half of the route or if it showed only the third left turn on the route. You do not decompose use cases into smaller pieces and call those pieces use cases. Likewise, a map does not group together all the left turns, then all the right turns, and then the straight segments and then call each of these groups a route. (Functional decomposition using use cases is a common mistake. We will discuss this later in this chapter.)

A use case depicts a *specific* scenario (or flow of events) that illustrates how the actor will use the system. A use case will typically have a main flow of events and also various alternate scenarios, just as a map depicts your main route but also shows other roads that could also be taken. Use cases do not specify all the possible ways to use the system. Otherwise, you would end up with the monolithic "Do Everything" use case (or a map of the entire world, showing all possible routes to the chosen destination).

How do you determine what the main and alternate scenarios are and how many alternates are needed? This is a judgment call you have to make based on the context of your system, what the actor wants to accomplish, and what is important to you. For example, in our earlier discussion on requirements in this chapter, we described two simple use case scenarios for ordering food at a restaurant, either of which could be the main scenario for an Order Meal use case. Which you would choose would depend on the context you have—is this a fast-food restaurant or a more traditional restaurant? As for the alternate flows, there could be many flows, slightly different yet still very similar, that accomplish ordering a meal—in one case, beverages may be ordered first and then the main meal, or the meal first and then beverages, and so forth. These are probably not the type of alternate scenarios you would want to capture (unless the sequence of ordering is important to you). But you probably would want to capture variants for situations such as when a customer requests a meal be prepared in a certain way, when you can't provide a certain meal because you have run out of a certain food, when you are offering special meals, when discounts are available, and so forth. You will want to capture alternate scenarios that are significant for your particular situation. What ties all these various flows together? They are all about accomplishing the specific outcome of the use case that the actor desires, in this case, ordering a meal.

Let's consider these key characteristics further. As discussed earlier, use cases should not be too small or too large. So, we have two initial boundaries for the scope of a use case (see Figure 3-2):

1. Use cases are not individual steps or functions.
2. Use cases do not contain every possible step that might ever be taken.

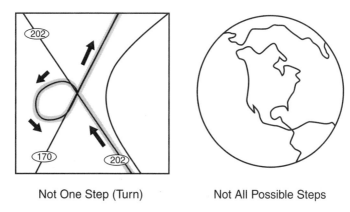

Not One Step (Turn)   Not All Possible Steps

Figure 3-2 *Use case scoping—boundaries.*

Within these two extremes, how do we know the proper scope for use cases? The first key characteristic you must keep in mind is to construct the use case in terms of *what* the system should do. This key characteristic immediately limits the scope of the use case because it eliminates all the "*hows*." Use cases should not describe how the scenario will be implemented. Again, we use the analogy of a map—at this point, you need to determine the requirements on the system (i.e., *what* the system must do), not the implementation (i.e., *how* the system will do it), just as a map shows *what* needs to be done (i.e., travel from point 1 to point 2) without showing *how* you should get there (e.g., by bus, train, automobile—see Figure 3-3).

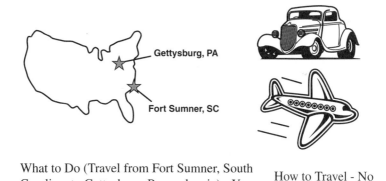

What to Do (Travel from Fort Sumner, South Carolina, to Gettysburg, Pennsylvania) - Yes   How to Travel - No

Figure 3-3 *Use case scoping—What must it do?*

As another example, let us consider an automotive diagnostics system used by an auto technician. The technician can perform many diagnostic actions on an automobile. The use case Compare Results To Compression Profile In Database is a use case that doesn't specify *what* needs to be done—it specifies *how* to do it (compare to the database). A better use case would be Evaluate Vehicle Compression (that's *what* needs to be done).

Another characteristic that limits the scope of a use case is taking the *actor's point of view*. This means use cases should be defined from the viewpoint of the actor that would use them, not from the system's viewpoint. The actor's viewpoint for use of a map is to "Determine a Route," not "Read Map Database," which is the viewpoint of a mapping software application (see Figure 3-4).

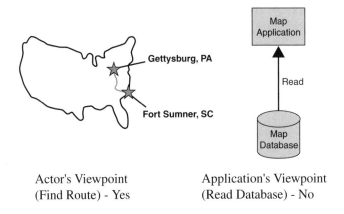

Actor's Viewpoint   Application's Viewpoint
(Find Route) - Yes   (Read Database) - No

Figure 3-4   *Use case scoping—Take the actor's point of view.*

In our auto diagnostics example, Provide Timing Information would be taking the system's point of view. The actor's point of view would be Test Vehicle Timing.

The next key characteristic is that use cases, with their actors, must capture an *entire flow* of events (a.k.a. a complete use case scenario) that will be performed. Today, autos have millions of lines of code onboard. So, the technician might use the diagnostics system to upload new software to the auto—but "upload new software" is *not* a use case. The upload is just one step in a larger flow that would contain actions such as getting the maintenance order, driving the auto into the proper service bay, making the proper electrical connections, discovering the current version of software that is onboard, querying for all software upgrades that are available and mandated, and performing the upload, not to mention conforming to any safety protocols along the way and so forth. A better use case might be Perform Software Maintenance Cycle. That use case scenario can include these or other steps.

Upload New Software is not an entire flow, and therefore is not a complete scenario. Each use case must portray the entire flow of how the actor(s) will use your system for a given scenario. This characteristic helps prevent the creation of single-step use cases, partial use cases, or functionally decomposed use cases (see Figure 3-5).

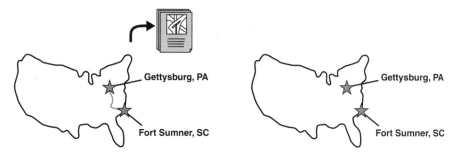

Entire Flow (Specifying Start and End Points [Fort Sumner, SC, and Gettysburg, PA], Calculating Route, Printing Map and Directions.) - Yes

Partial Flow (Only Specifying Start and End Points - Fort Sumner, SC, and Gettysburg, PA) - No

Figure 3-5   *Use case scoping—Create an entire flow.*

But the use case can't just be any collection of steps. The last key characteristic is that the use case must provide some recognizable *value* to its actors. In our example, raising the automobile on a lift provides no value on its own. However, when we add draining the oil, replacing the oil filter, adding new oil, and bringing the auto back down (i.e., doing the entire oil change), then we have described something of value. Likewise, a map may be extremely accurate, but if it doesn't cover the area you are interested in or doesn't provide a route to your destination, it provides no value (see Figure 3-6).

Value to the Actor - Producing This
Route Has Value to the Actor (the Route
from Ft. Sumner to Gettysburg). - Yes

Finding the Location of Lincoln,
Nebraska, Has No Value to This Actor. - No

Figure 3-6   *Use case scoping—Provide value for the actor.*

Watch Out—Peace, Love, and Harmony

Be careful not to get derailed by the argument that "everything has some
inherent value"—that each step in a use case is necessary and therefore
is valuable in some way. Although this might be a loving, harmonious
life philosophy, it is an imprudent way to build use cases. For example,
although raising the automobile might be necessary to change the oil, it
does not mean that raising the auto adds value. In other words, it might
be *necessary* to raise the auto, but that step alone is not *sufficient* to
add value.

When creating use case scenarios, if you are having difficulty with the idea of
value, you might want to look at one of the other key characteristics—taking
the actor's point of view. If the technician only raised the automobile on a lift,
drained the oil, and removed the oil filter, would the customer (another actor)
be satisfied? No, she came to get an oil *change*, not to get an oil *drain*. If you
are not sure, try asking the real person who will eventually be that actor.
When you have the opportunity to ask the users, do so; this can help you
avoid career-limiting mistakes.

From the Real World—No Good Deed Goes Unpunished

A programmer whose expertise was in graphical user interfaces (GUIs)
and human-machine interface standards was hired at a company I worked
for. One of the first projects he worked on was a little piece of software

that had been used by three departments to provide its users with a certain extraction of data from a corporate database. This was one of those homegrown applications that is never really formally specified, designed, or tested. Instead, one department had an immediate need, and somebody cobbled together this application. The other two departments saw it later and wanted to use it too, so they each took a copy. Naturally, the three copies diverged over time. Nothing was really wrong with this application, but it did have slightly different GUIs for each department, which made maintenance of the software three times as costly when compared to having a single interface. The newly hired programmer understood this and noted that the interfaces did not comply with good GUI practices and standards.

So, he thought he would be proactive and remedy this situation. He unified the three GUIs and brought them up to proper standards regarding presentation and user interaction. Unfortunately, he did not bother to ask the real-world users if that was what they wanted. The wrath of three departments rained down on this poor fellow, who was only doing what he thought was best. His error was that he *assumed* he knew what was best for the users without asking them. In other words, the changes he made did not provide *value* to these users.

The "WAVE" Test

A simple way to validate that you are on the right track with your use cases is to use the "WAVE" tests. [NAIB1] The WAVE acronym captures the essence of the previously mentioned characteristics:

W	Does the use case describe **W**hat to do, not how to do it?
A	Is the use case described from the **A**ctor's point of view?
V	Does the use case include **V**alue for the actor?
E	Is the flow of events an **E**ntire scenario?

The WAVE tests are a great way to keep yourself on track when creating new use cases, and they are also useful for checking your set of candidate use cases afterward to validate that they are proper. If they pass the WAVE test, you are well on your way to success with properly scoped use cases (see Figure 3-7) and have avoided the major flaws often seen in use case models.

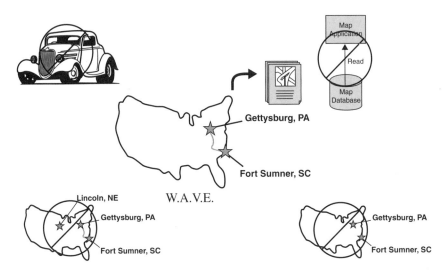

Figure 3-7   *Use case scoping—Well scoped use case.*

One Last Sanity Check

One final way to evaluate that you have properly scoped your system use cases is to count how many you have. The number of use cases in the largest systems should number in the "tens" range, not the "hundreds." Simple systems might have less than ten use cases. So, if you have a very high use case count, and you are not building a very large, complex system, you should reassess the scope of your project and your use cases against the criteria discussed earlier in this chapter.

Actors

So, who uses these use cases? In Chapter 2, we discussed business actors. They are the people, companies, or systems that come to do business with you. That was at the business modeling level of *abstraction*. Now that we are at the requirements elicitation/specification phase, we merely refer to *actors*. Actors are the people or things that interact with your system (that will be created to implement those business processes). They are not specific people. They represent a *role* that the actor (person or system) plays with respect to your system.

For example, "Mary" would not be a proper actor. If you wanted to include what Mary does in your models, you would ask, "What does she do (i.e., what role does she play)?" If she is Head of Security, the actor could be "Security Chief"—this is the role she plays within the system.

Deep Dive—Who's on First

An actor can also represent a *set of roles* that interact with your system. This actor can interact differently with the different use cases it interacts with. At first blush, this may be puzzling. Previously, we said an actor is a role. So, it now sounds like we are saying that a role can represent a set of roles. Indeed, that is correct. Looking at our example, when you ask, "What does Mary do?," you answer that she is Security Chief. You might stop there, depending on the type of system you are creating. However, Security Chief is the type of role that really can have many roles within it. (Note that this situation is especially true when the actor name really describes a job title.) So, if you ask again, "What does the Security Chief do?," you may find that the Security Chief has many roles. She may act as a manager, a guard, a driver, and so forth (see Figure 3-8).

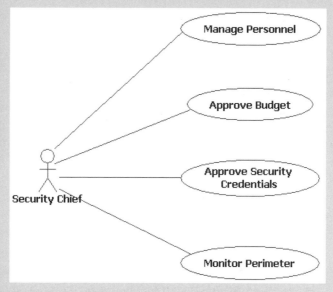

Figure 3-8 *Actor—Security Chief.*

However, although you can depict multiple roles in this manner, it's not really explicit what the additional roles are. Those roles are implicit in the combination of the actor and which use case it is performing. A clearer, more explicit way to depict roles with multiple roles is to use a generalization relationship. Generalizations are often referred to as the

continues

Deep Dive—Who's on First (*continued*)

"is a" relationship. Referring to Figure 3-9, we see that the Security Chief "is a" manager (shown by the association with an empty arrowhead). The Security Chief also "is a" guard. As you can see, the use of generalizations between actors can more clearly depict the various roles a Security Chief may perform.

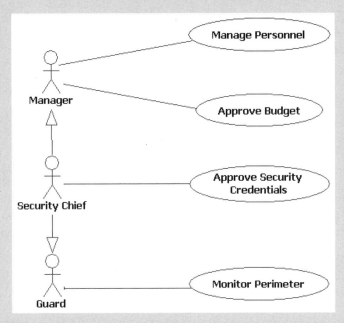

Figure 3-9   *Actors and generalization.*

This diagram tells us that the Security Chief can approve security credentials. A guard cannot (a guard is *not* a Security Chief), nor can a manager. Now because the Security Chief "is a" guard, the Security Chief can also do what the guards do; that is, the Security Chief can also monitor the perimeter. Because the Security Chief is a manager, she may also manage personnel and approve budgets.

Deep Dive—Nothing Unreal Exists

Although actors typically are the people and systems that your systems interact with, there is one type of "actor" that is a bit unusual. Certain events can be actors. For example, natural disasters, a change in monetary exchange rates, power failures, or simply the passage of time can be actors. Your typical actors consciously use your system for a purpose (i.e., the value your use cases provide). Obviously, events such as a power failure are not conscious, nor can they get value from a use case. So why are they considered actors? They perform one important function like typical actors do—they initiate use cases. When monetary exchange rates change, that event might trigger a use case that changes a brokerage firm's trading limits on commodities. A lightning strike could trigger a use case that initiates backup power systems.

Should all events be modeled as actors? Obviously not. Run of the mill events, such as a software error condition or a user selecting a product to purchase online, are not the type of events that rise to the stature of an actor. The events that can be represented as actors are, like typical actors, external to the system. They are also significant enough that you have created use cases to handle such events. As with many gray areas of systems design, common sense can be your guide if all else fails. Ask yourself the questions: Does depicting the event as an actor communicate an important aspect of your system design? Does it make sense?

Use Case Relationships

Use cases interact with more than actors—they can have relationships with other use cases. Let's say you are developing a use case around a driver taking an automobile on a drive. For discussion purposes, let us say that the basic use case, Take Trip, has the basic flow of planning the trip, fueling the car, driving to the destination, sightseeing, and driving home. This use case could have many different alternate scenarios. As you develop other use cases, you'll note that one thing is always included in the scenarios—fueling the auto. The act of fueling the auto is the same across the use cases. This common behavior can be represented with a special association, as shown in Figure 3-10, as a dashed arrow labeled with "<<include>>."

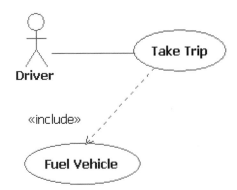

Figure 3-10 *Include relationship.*

The *include* association means that the *included use case* behavior (Fuel Vehicle) is inserted in the flow of the *base use case* (Take Trip). Use cases that are included are use cases that are reusable—common to many use cases. Even though they are common, included use cases are also mandatory. In this example, the base use case, Take Trip, is incomplete without its included use case, Fuel Vehicle. When the base scenario reaches the *inclusion point* in the flow where Fuel Vehicle is to be included (as specified in the base use case scenario), the Fuel Vehicle use case is executed.

As mentioned, there could be many alternate scenarios for Take Trip. Many different *optional* behaviors could be added to the base scenario. For a longer trip, you might want to stop for a meal. This can be represented with a dashed arrow labeled with "<<extend>>" as in Figure 3-11.

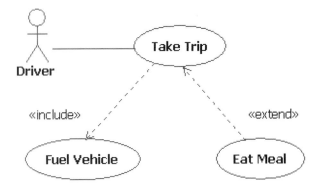

Figure 3-11 *Extend relationship.*

The *extend* association means that the base use case (Take Trip) can be extended with the optional *extending use case* (Eat Meal). An extending use case actually changes the flow of the base use case. Whether the extending use case behavior is executed is based on a decision point in the main flow. In this case, when the base scenario reaches the *extension point* in the flow where the Eat Meal option might be taken, the driver must decide whether he wants to eat. If so, Eat Meal would be executed. If not, the base flow would continue.

Unlike the include relationship, which inserts behavior at a single point in the flow, an extend relationship can change the base use case flow at multiple places. For example, let's say that one alternate flow of Take Trip includes photographing the interesting sites. So, we add an extending use case, Photograph Sites (see Figure 3-12).

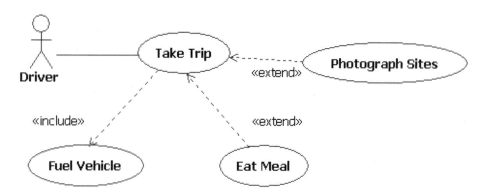

Figure 3-12 *Extend relationship—Photograph Sites has multiple extension points.*

We can define Photograph Sites so that when the decision point is reached and the driver decides to take photos, the base use case will be altered at numerous specified points with various behaviors. In this example, not only will the Photograph Sites use case extend the base behavior to take photos after sightseeing, but it also will extend behavior later in the trip's base flow to stop at the film processing store and drop off the film to have pictures made.

The include and extend relationships are similar in some ways yet different in others. The significant differences are summarized in Table 3-1.

Table 3-1   *Key Differences Between Include and Extend Relationships*

	Included Use Case	**Extending Use Case**
Is this use case optional?	No	Yes
Is the base use case complete without this use case?	No	Yes
Is the execution of this use case conditional?	No	Yes
Does this use case change the behavior of the base use case?	No	Yes

Includes and extends are useful tools to help you structure your use case models—includes to identify common use cases and extends to simplify complex scenarios. However, remember the most important task is to properly define and elaborate your use case scenarios. Don't get bogged down by focusing on includes and extends instead of building good use cases.

Watch Out—Pandora's Box

Although the include and extend relationships have positive value in modeling, their misuse has opened a Pandora's Box of problems on software projects. Some are as follows:

1. Violation of basic use case principles. When some folks use includes and extends, they violate the WAVE principles. For example, instead of the base use case being an entire flow, they will put part of the flow in the base, the next part in an included use case, and the third part of the flow in an additional base use case. (In our Take Trip example, using this incorrect approach, Take Trip would just be Drive to Fuel Station, and then the Fuel Vehicle use case would be included. Then, a new use case would be added: Drive to Restaurant, and so forth.) The justification they use is that all of them together make up the entire scenario. That is not valid. Remember to stick to the use case basics.

2. An extending use case for all possible alternate paths. The extend relationship is not intended to be used to capture every possible error condition that might occur in your system. Although major or critical error conditions might be acceptable extensions, trivial ones, such as when the user does not make a selection on an input form where a selection is required, should be left to program design. If not,

you might either end up in "analysis paralysis" or have a use case model that is completely unintelligible and unwieldy.

3. Degradation into a functional decomposition approach. (If you are not familiar with this, functional decomposition is an analysis technique used in some structured analysis and design approaches wherein you decompose the system into smaller and smaller pieces along functional lines.) This misuse is not unexpected because use cases are functional in nature, and use case diagrams are much like the context diagrams of some structured design techniques. Be very wary of this error. This is such a common problem that it has now been elevated to "anti-pattern" status in the industry. (An anti-pattern "…describes a commonly occurring solution to a problem that generates decidedly negative consequences." [BROW1]) A functionally decomposed system that is intended to be implemented in an object-oriented manner will typically give you few of the benefits of object orientation. You will notice when you are on this path because a functionally decomposed system will quickly begin to violate the WAVE principles—your use cases will not be entire flows, will lose their actor focus each will not be providing value, and so forth.

One real-world example of taking this to the extreme was a software designer who wanted to create use cases of such fine granularity that each use case was a single function. Her rationale was that she would then be able to refactor and recombine the use cases however she needed. This is not the intention of use cases or of refactoring. (Refactoring is a technique intended for "…improving the design of the code after it has been written." [FOWL1]) As her system had not been written yet, she instead should have chosen to design it correctly in the first place. This is an example of what I call the "Design by Book Club" approach, where people want to use the latest development technique for everything they do, irrespective of its applicability.

4. Confusion and misuse of include and extend. This is a case where people do not understand the basic semantics of the two relationships; that is, they do not understand the differences noted in Table 3-1 (also see "Topics to Consider—Visibility"). The use of the UML as a common notation with common meaning offers great benefits that can be destroyed by misusing the notation.

As mentioned earlier, do not use the include and extend relationships as architectural tools. Use them primarily to simplify and clarify your use case models.

Use Case Specifications

We've talked repeatedly of how a use case should specify a complete flow of events. So, what form should that specification take? One is a type of UML *interaction diagram* called a *sequence diagram* (we will discuss these later in this chapter). The other is a textual specification of what the use case does, typically called a use case specification.

The use case specification is a structured, textual document that describes the use case scenario in natural language. An example is seen in Figure 3-13. This example is from a fictitious Online Medical Records system. It describes one use case for recovering archived clinical records (in this context, "records" refers to all the medical information about a person under care, not to individual database records).

There are many formats for use case specifications, and you should tailor them to your specific needs. Figure 3-13 contains key information that should be included in your spec: name, short purpose, contact and change information, *pre-conditions* that must be true for the use case to execute, *post-conditions* that must be true after the use case is run, known limitations, and assumptions. This is followed by the basic flow. The basic flow is the "good day" scenario where everything goes as planned. Alternate scenarios are also documented. The alternate scenarios describe how the use case flow can be altered based on a specific condition. If the alternate flow is captured in another use case related to the main use case through an extends association, where that extension occurs in the specification is identified by an *extension point*. Similarly, if this use case included other use cases (an include relationship), we would identify this by using an *inclusion point* for each use case.

As you can see, use case specifications are intentionally short—no more than a few pages. The intent is to succinctly capture the flow of the use case. If it gets too large, your use case might be trying to do more than it should be doing, or you might be getting bogged down in trivial alternate flows.

Use Case Description

Use Case Name: Unarchive Clinical Records

Use Case Purpose: The purpose of this use case is to recover Clinical Records from the archive.

Point of Contact: Jan Tarmand

Date Modified: 11/29/03

Pre-Conditions: None Identified

Post-Conditions: The Records Closure Schedule and Records Destruction Schedule may be updated.

Limitations: The Clinical Records to be recovered are specified by Resident name.

Assumptions: Clinical Records are to be closed 14 days after the Resident leaves the facility.

Basic Flow:

    A.   The Archive is locked against update.

    B.   The specified Clinical Record is searched for in the Records Destruction Schedule

    C.   Extension Point—Condition 1

    D.   The Record Destruction Schedule is updated to remove the requested Clinical Record from the Schedule.

    E.   The specified Clinical Record is recovered from the Archive

    F.   Extension Point—Condition 2

    G.   If the Resident has left the facility, the Record Closure Schedule is updated to schedule the Clinical Record for closure.

    H.   Archive is closed and exclusive access is released.

Alternate Flows:

Condition Triggering Alternate Flow:

Condition 1: The specified record is not found in the Record Destruction Schedule.

    C1.   An error message is displayed to the user and is also logged, indicating the Specific Clinical Record was not found in the Record Destruction Schedule.

    C2.   Step H in the Basic Flow is then executed.

Condition Triggering Alternate Flow:

Condition 2: The specified record is not found in the Archive.

    F1.   An error message is displayed to the user and is also logged, indicating the Specific Clinical Record was not found in the Archive.

    F2.   Step H in the Basic Flow is then executed.

Figure 3-13 *Use case specification. [NAIB2]*

Text-based use case specifications have several benefits:

1. Simple to use; no CASE tools required.
2. No methodology knowledge required.
3. No training needed.
4. Portable.
5. Can be done anytime and anywhere.
6. Can express the use case in the customer's language.

These characteristics make these specifications ideal for working with your nontechnical stakeholders (e.g., customers, business sponsors).

From the Real World—Let Mikey Do It! Yeah!

I was working on one project as part of a very small team that was to introduce use cases into a project development team to establish the customer requirements. We began to work with our business sponsors, who were very busy and had little time to dedicate to us. We met weekly and tried to elicit the system requirements with a use case approach. This worked well, but as there were so few of us actually creating the use cases, work was progressing slowly, so we decided to take a different approach. We gave our business sponsors a two-day introduction to use cases—what they meant, the symbols, how to draw the diagrams, and the use case specification format. We also did a few problems together to give them some hands-on experience. In our next meeting, we brainstormed all the use cases they thought we would have to create. Then, instead of sitting through the weekly meeting trying to slog through each use case with the whole group, we merely asked them to fill out the use case spec for the use cases that fell in their area of expertise. This approach worked beautifully! The business people did a fine job with the specifications, and we were freed up to do other tasks on the project.

Specifying use cases in text has one significant drawback. They suffer from the same weakness as all textual specifications: when they get more complex, you cannot easily understand all the relationships and interactions. This is where the strength of the UML sequence diagram lies.

Review of Sequence Diagram Basics

You will recall that in Chapter 2, we introduced sequence diagrams. To review, a sequence diagram shows the interactions between the model elements for a given scenario in time order (time runs vertically down the page). The arrows on this diagram indicate the messages that flow between the various model elements. The dashed lines that run vertically below the model elements are called *lifelines*. Lifelines show the existence of the model element. The sequence diagram for the use case specified in Figure 3-13 can be seen in Figure 3-14.

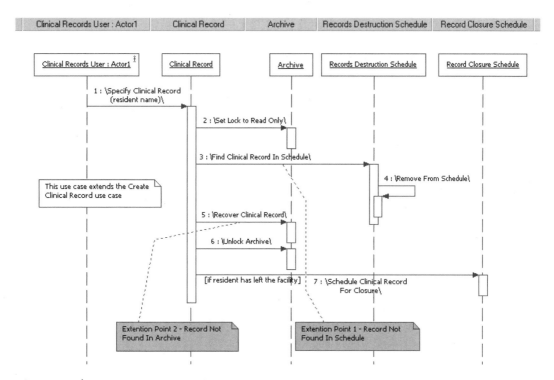

Figure 3-14　*Unarchive Medical Record sequence diagram.*

More on Sequence Diagrams

We used a few additional elements in this sequence diagram. You can see we used "notes" (the rectangular symbol with a folded-over corner, which can be used on any diagram type) as one way to indicate where any extension points are. Such notes can also be used to "link" sequence diagrams together. This is especially useful for long sequences or to link to the sequence diagrams for included or extending use cases. Also, one way you can use conditions on messages is shown on message 7 in Figure 3-14 (in brackets). Some additional notations you might see are in Figure 3-15.

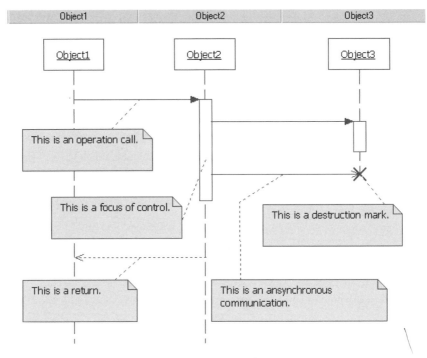

Figure 3-15 *Additional sequence diagram elements.*

Here, we use notes to identify different diagram elements. We have seen previously the *operation call*, shown as an arrow with a solid, filled-in arrowhead. When such calls are made, control is passed to the element on the arrowhead end of the message. You can see the scope (duration) of such control by the *focus of control* bar. This is the rectangular bar on the lifeline, which indicates when this element (or a subordinate element) is performing processing. A message that does not transfer control is the *asynchronous message*, show as a line with an "open," sticklike arrowhead. When this type of message is sent, the sending element continues on with its processing.

On the end of this particular asynchronous message is a *destruction marker*, the large "X" on the lifeline. (You might hear this referred to as a "*Stop*" per UML 2.0.) This indicates when that instance of the object is destroyed. Last, as we saw in Chapter 2, a *return* message is represented as a dashed arrow. These indicate a return from a called operation. Return messages are optional because if you showed every return, the sequence diagram would become quite cluttered. Use them for key, meaningful returns only.

We have found that the sequence diagram is the most generally useful of all the UML diagrams. Not only can they clearly depict the flow of use case scenarios, but they also can do the following:

- Provide control flow information.
- Depict database transactions (as a transaction map showing the initiating user role and all the entities that are touched during the transaction).
- Identify key parameters that must be shared among elements of your system.
- Give insight into the creation and destruction of objects in your system.
- Show when an object might be doing too much. (Does one of your objects send most of the messages out and thus control the entire application? Was that intended?)
- Indicate when the design might have performance issues. (Does one of your objects receive most of the messages and thus become a performance bottleneck?).
- Provide an easy, visual way for users to validate the steps they really take (or want to take) and in what order.

Topics to Consider

You might want to examine these additional topics:

- Use cases and the generalization relationship. Generalization is the third type of association that can occur between use cases (along with include and extend). What does it mean when one use case "is another" use case? What would a child use case *inherit* from its parent use case?

• Explore visibility, includes, and extends. Using the include and extend relationships has semantic implications to visibility of the base use case into the included or extending use case (and vice versa).

Terms

Requirements	Desirements
Scope creep	Role
Functional requirements	Nonfunctional requirements
Use case	Actor
Generalization	Abstraction
WAVE test	Pandora
Functional decomposition	Anti-pattern
Global positioning system	Refactoring
Include relationship	Extend relationship
Inclusion point	Extension point
Base use ccase	Extending use case
Included use case	Alternate flow
Interaction diagram	Sequence diagram
Lifeline	Focus of control
Asynchronous message	Return message
Destruction mark	Stop

Summary

We began this chapter with a discussion of what requirements are and just how important it is in real life, not just system development, to create and understand your requirements. You learned the unfortunate consequences (both personal and project-related) of not attending to requirements first. We also noted the various types of requirements.

From there, we moved on to discuss how to model requirements using UML. We revisited use cases, and you learned the key characteristics your use cases must have in order to be created properly. We also revisited actors and talked about generalizing their roles. We briefly mentioned some unusual actors such as time and earthquakes and how to use such events as actors.

We also covered new ground on the relationships that can exist between use cases. There, you learned the key differences between the include and extend relationships and how they alter the flow of use cases. You were also warned of the various pitfalls of these relationships. We provided a template and guidance on how to create good use case specifications.

Lastly, we reviewed sequence diagrams, and you saw how they provide a different and important view of use case scenarios that complements the textual use case specifications. We also introduced some new UML elements that you might encounter in sequence diagrams.

Review Questions

1. True or False: Changes in requirements are expected and do not significantly impact the success of projects.

2. True or False: The cost to repair defects increases linearly over the lifecycle of a project.

3. "The system shall provide redundant backup of all data" is a:
   a. Nonfunctional requirement
   b. Functional requirement
   c. Combination of a.) and b.)
   d. None of the above

4. When discussing the domain of laundering your clothes, would the following be good use cases? If not, give at least one reason why not.
   a. Add Detergent
   b. Wash Clothes
   c. Agitate Laundry

5. Actors can:

     a. Depict a single role

     b. Depict multiple roles

     c. Not depict any roles

     d. All of the above

     e. Both a.) and b.)

     f. None of the above

6. True or False: An included use case inserts its flow at a single point in the base use case.

7. True or False: The flow of an extending use case must always be executed.

8. True or False: The flow of a base use case is complete even without any of its possible extending use cases.

[BASE1] For more information, see the following:

> Basel II: http://www2.ifc.org/syndications/pdfs/Basel2/Overview_NewBaselCapitalAccord_April03_engl.pdf.

> Sarbanes Oxley Act: http://www.sec.gov/divisions/corpfin/faqs/soxact2002.htm.

> FDA 21 CFR Part 11: http://www.fda.gov/ohrms/dockets/dockets/00d1540/00d-1540-mm00027-04.pdf.

[BROW1] Brown, William J., Raphael Malveau, Hays McCormick, and Thomas Mowbray. 1998. *Antipatterns: Refactoring Software, Architectures, and Projects in Crisis*. John Wiley & Sons.

[DORF1] Dorfmann, Merlin, and Thayer. 1990. *Standards, Guidelines, and Examples of System and Software Requirements Engineering*. IEEE Computer Society Press.

[FOWL1] Fowler, Martin, Kent Beck, John Brant, William Opdyke, and Don Roberts. 1999. *Refactoring: Improving the Design of Existing Code*. Addison-Wesley.

[GABB1] Gabb, Andrew, ed. 2001. *Requirements Categorization*. (Prepared by the Requirements Working Group of the International Council on Systems Engineering. For information purposes only. Not approved by INCOSE Technical Board. Not an official position of INCOSE.)

[LEFF2] Leffingwell, Dean and Don Widrig. 2000. *Managing Software Requirements: A Unified Approach*. Boston: Addison-Wesley.

[NAIB1] Naiburg, Eric J. and Robert A. Maksimchuk. 2001. *UML for Database Design*. Boston, MA: Addison-Wesley.

[NAIB2] Adapted from a use case specification by Naiburg, Eric J. and Robert A. Maksimchuk. 2001. *UML for Database Design*. Boston, MA: Addison-Wesley.

4

Architectural Modeling

Topics Covered in This Chapter

What Is Architecture?

Why Model Architecture?

Logical Architecture

      Class Diagrams

      Systems and Subsystems

Physical Architecture

      Component Diagrams

      Deployment Diagrams

Architectural Patterns

What Is Model Driven Architecture?

Topics to Consider

Terms

Summary

Review Questions

Introduction

In this chapter, you will learn the different types of architectural models you can build using the UML and how to describe them visually. Modeling architectures is currently one of the most popular uses of the UML. Because a robust architecture is the key to a successful application, especially with respect to a long lifespan for the application and its need to exist and change over time, modeling provides the critical ability to understand, communicate, and validate your architectural designs. As this chapter continues, you will understand the different levels of architecture, including business, application, and enterprise.

What Is Architecture?

In a conversation we once had with Grady Booch, he said, "Every software system has an architecture, regardless of whether the architecture was developed intentionally. The bigger question is whether it is a good architecture."

The textbook definition of architecture is

> Architecture:
> 1. The art or science of building; *specifically*: the art or practice of designing and building structures and especially habitable ones.
> 1a: Formation or construction as or as if as the result of conscious act <the architecture of the garden>.
> 2. The manner in which the components of a computer or computer system are organized and integrated. [MEWE1]

An architecture depicts how something's parts come together to form a whole. An airplane has an architecture; this book has an architecture—even your body has an architecture, although their characteristics vary. If you are going to build something, it is quite helpful to describe its architecture, either textually, as in the outline of a book before writing it, or by modeling what that thing will look like (see Figure 4-1).

For the purposes of this book, an architecture is the structure of a system. The architecture incorporates the business rules, the software, and how the software will communicate with other pieces of software. An architecture can include software both inside and outside of your organization. Because your internal systems might need to be integrated with partners, customers, and vendors, your architecture can be made up of internal and external systems. It also can include the hardware on which the software runs, and it might even include an understanding and description of who will use the system and how it will be used.

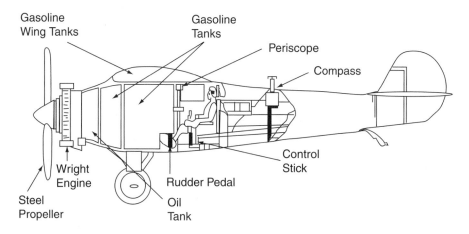

Figure 4-1 *A partial view of an airplane's architectural drawing.*

Why Model Architecture?

As discussed in Chapters 1 and 2, modeling software and systems architectures is quite valuable. It helps you to understand how the system is to be developed and constructed. Software is often made up of many pieces, generally called components, which interface with each other to execute business logic and sometimes to exchange data. Being able to understand how that architecture functions and where dependencies exist across the system can make the life of everyone involved in the software development process easier and help you design a better system. By modeling the architecture, you provide a great mechanism for communicating the architecture to others, breaking it down into different timelines for development, understanding interdependencies with other systems or organizations, distributing the workload, looking for poor patterns or designs, and much more.

Visually modeling the architecture of software or systems provides many valuable benefits. A visual model gives you a direct look at what you are planning to build before you start to build it physically. This enables you to understand the plan and communicate its designs. It gives you a way to look at the designs to ensure they make sense in the context of the overall architecture. Often designers consider only the architecture of the part of the system they are working on and miss the bigger picture—that their components must fit together with others to form the overall system.

You can model the architecture of software and systems at three main levels: the enterprise level, the system level, and the software level.

Enterprise Architecture

An enterprise architecture is designed to give a high-level visualization of the enterprise, including business processes, organizational structures, systems (including hardware and software that are in place), and desired evolution of the existing architecture. You can base your architecture on a variety of different architectural frameworks, including the Zachman Framework, the Federal Enterprise Architecture Framework (FEAF), the Department of Defense Architecture Framework (DoDAF) and others specific to various organizations or industries. These enterprise architecture frameworks provide a standard way to model the enterprise architecture to ensure consistency across the organization with everyone else who is modeling the enterprise.

From the Real World—Mandated Enterprise Architectures

The United States Federal Government has mandated that all government agencies have an enterprise architecture to show how the agency uses software and hardware, as well as how it operates from a business perspective. The Office of Management and Budget (OMB) has put into place a standard framework called the Federal Enterprise Architecture Framework (FEAF) that each of the agencies must follow. Although there is a framework in place as to how the agencies should capture the enterprise architecture, which includes both modeling and documentation, there is still room for interpretation. Because the FEAF is a set of reference models, or more accurately, meta-models, each agency interprets it a little bit differently, but at least they are following the same process for building their enterprise architecture.

One piece of legislation, the Clinger-Cohen Act, mandates the use of enterprise architectures to improve the system integration between agencies and reduce the duplication of efforts and systems within agencies. To ensure that the enterprise architecture is built, the OMB will not provide continued funding unless the agency can demonstrate that it is creating the enterprise architecture.

We were working with one particular agency that had to show to the United States Congress UML models of their enterprise architecture to demonstrate that it was under construction and to provide the status of their agency's progress. Using these UML models of the enterprise, the two groups were able to communicate with each other about the software applications that existed within the agency and the business processes being performed by the agency. Thus, they could build a realistic plan for modernizing the agency over the coming years.

This proved that an enterprise architecture can effectively document the state of the enterprise as it is today, provide an understanding of how you want it to evolve over time, and give a plan or blueprint for how you want to evolve the architecture. It is quite important to ensure that the enterprise architecture is a living document that evolves through time and not something that is only created once and never changed.

Lessons Learned

1. Providing a view of your enterprise architecture to others helps to ensure interoperability across organizations.

2. Building an enterprise architecture helps you understand what exists within your organization, including software, hardware, business processes, and organizational resources.

3. An enterprise architecture must be an evolving document. It cannot be built once and ignored; rather, it must be changed as the enterprise changes.

4. An enterprise architecture must be a combination of models and documents to ensure a complete understanding of the enterprise by those who need to understand it.

System Architecture

Generally, a system is made up of multiple software programs that run on a piece of hardware or that control that hardware by causing it to perform some sort of action. For example, an airplane is a large piece of hardware that is run by many different software programs. When combined, the hardware and software form the complete system—the airplane. Similarly, manufacturers of DVD players combine many different pieces of hardware with software that enables the different hardware components to work together as one system: the DVD player.

Unlike a software architecture, which usually looks at a particular application, a system architecture looks at all parts of the system. It includes both the software and hardware components and provides a visualization of how they work together. The system architecture is one of the most important architectures to model in system development. A pacemaker, for example, is composed of different parts that perform different actions to keep a heart working correctly. Each of these pieces is run by software, but more importantly, the overall architecture of the pacemaker ensures that the pieces are working together to perform the correct actions. Although each hardware component may work independently, they also rely on the other parts of the pacemaker and the software that directs the operation of each of those parts. Modeling the architecture of the system to ensure that both the hardware and software are understood helps to ensure that it will be designed correctly and that any interdependencies are understood and are built to work effectively.

Software Architecture

A software architecture model enables the visualization of the software designs as they are intended to be actually implemented. When designing software, multiple components or pieces generally have to be interfaced to make up the overall application. By modeling the software architecture, you can visualize how the different components that make up the application fit together to share functions, data, and business processes. Although an enterprise architecture ties directly to the business needs, the software architecture does so indirectly by specifying a software design that complies to the enterprise architecture. A software architect might use business models to help him determine how to design the software, but these designs aren't generally included directly as part of the software architecture itself.

Logical Architecture

We just discussed the various scopes that an architecture can have (i.e., enterprise, system, and software architectures). Various levels of abstraction also exist for such architectures, each containing a different level of detail about the architecture. The two levels of abstraction we will discuss are logical architecture and physical architecture.

A logical architecture represents an architecture that is independent of the overall technology to be implemented. It is an interpretation of what that architecture should look like. It is not intended to show the implementation software, but rather an abstraction of it. In software, the logical architecture normally denotes a description of the software's architecture in plain language (nontechnical). It is not optimized for any specific technology (it is technology-independent). Architects, not typical developers, often create these logical architectures.

Contrasting the various logical architectures, the enterprise architecture shows how the organization works and the intended direction in which the company is going. The system architecture shows how the system to be developed will meet those business needs. And the software logical architecture depicts the structure of the software executing within that system.

Class Diagrams

Using the UML, you design a logical architecture using classes in a class diagram. A class is visualized as a box containing two horizontal lines. Above the first line is the class's name, which is the logical description of the class and is typically a noun. Examples of a class name are Customer, Employee, and Order, as shown in Figure 4-2.

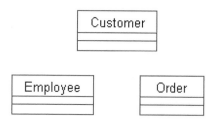

Figure 4-2   *Classes on a class diagram.*

Attributes of a class are shown above the second line in the class and are used to describe the different properties of that class. They provide additional detail pertaining to that class. Attributes have additional properties attached to them that describe the type of data that we intend to capture within that attribute. Examples of some attribute types are Number, String (textual information), Boolean (yes or no), and Date. The type is displayed on a UML class to the right of the attribute name, as shown in Figure 4-3.

Operations, which you will see in figures later in this chapter (such as Figure 4-11), appear on a class below the second line and are used to indicate the behavior of a class. Operations define the logic that will execute in the system, both basic (e.g., returning an error) and sophisticated (e.g., a large algorithmic calculation). We will cover operations in more depth later in this chapter.

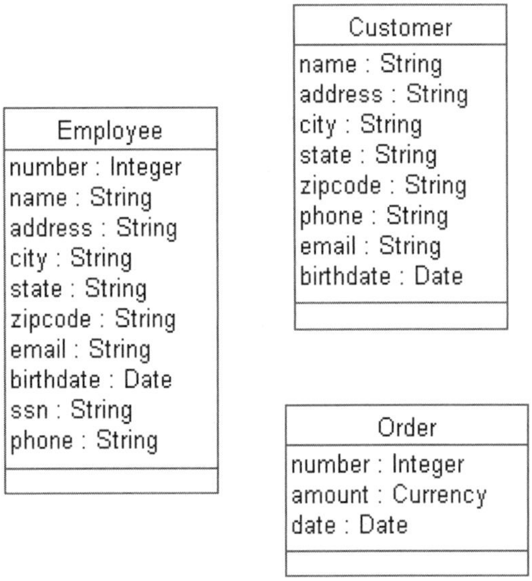

Employee

Employee
number : Integer
name : String
address : String
city : String
state : String
zipcode : String
email : String
birthdate : Date
ssn : String
phone : String

Customer
name : String
address : String
city : String
state : String
zipcode : String
phone : String
email : String
birthdate : Date

Order
number : Integer
amount : Currency
date : Date

Figure 4-3   *Classes with attributes.*

You can use different types of associations in a class diagram to show relationships between classes or between classes and other modeling elements. Figure 4-4 shows the different types of associations and gives a brief definition of each.

When defining an association, you can also designate each class's multiplicity. Multiplicity is used to show the number of objects that participate in the association. Multiplicity can be defined on an association and is shown on each end of the association. There are many combinations of multiplicity annotations. Here are some examples:

1	Exactly one
0..*	Zero or more
1..*	One or more
0..1	Zero or one
3..9	Specified range (3, 4, 5, 6, 7, 8, or 9)

Name	Graphic	Description
Undirectional Association	———————⟶	A relationship between two model elements that is navigated in primarily a single direction
Bidirectional Association	———————	A relationship between two model elements that is navigated in both directions
Dependency	— — — —⟶	A relationship between two model elements where a change to one may cause a change to the other
Aggregation	———⟶◇	A relationship between two model elements indicating that one is part of the other
Composite Aggregation	———⟶◆	An aggregation where both model elements are tightly coupled to the point that the child cannot exist without the parent
Generalization	———————▷	A relationship between model elements indicating that one element (subclass) is a "kind of" another element (superclass)

Figure 4-4   *Association descriptions.*

Multiplicity can be defined as a specific number, as "many" (meaning an unlimited number can occur), or as a range, such as 0 to 6. Figure 4-5 shows the classes from Figure 4-3 with associations and multiplicity added.

In Figure 4-5, the association between Employee and Customer is read as "an Employee is associated with 0 or more Customers, and a Customer is associated with 1 or more Employees." You can also add a role to each end of the association to better define it. In Figure 4-6, roles are added to our example.

As you may notice, there is a plus sign (+) before the rolename. No, that isn't a typo; it does belong there. The plus sign defines the role as public when used in the definition of code. A role can be public (+), protected (#), private (-), or implementation where no adornment exists. Public means that the role is accessible to all elements that need to access it, protected is only available to those elements that are part of the relation and elements it is related to, private is only available to that association, and implementation means it is only available to the overall package that implements that role.

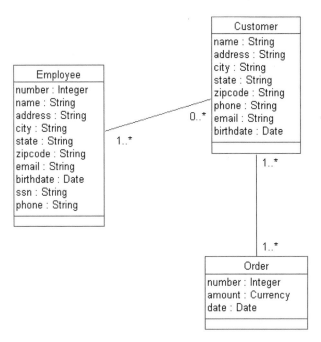

Figure 4-5   *Class diagram with associations.*

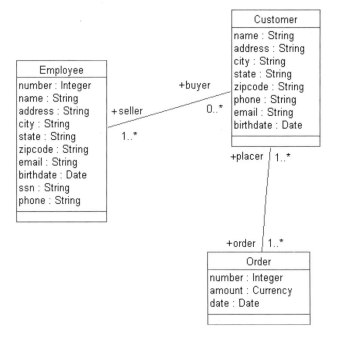

Figure 4-6   *Class diagram with association and roles.*

When creating a logical architecture model, generalizations are used to show how classes have a hierarchy of definition. For example, an employee can be either fulltime or part-time. When defining an Employee class, you might want to provide additional attributes to capture these different types of employees. But, an Employee class might be more clearly understood by nontechnical reviewers as being various types of employees, as seen in Figure 4-7. This indicates that both fulltime and part-time employees inherit all the attributes and operations of the parent Employee class.

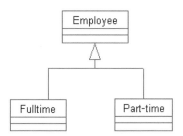

Figure 4-7 *Generalization.*

Systems and Subsystems

In this section, we will introduce a new UML construct called a *stereotype*. A stereotype enables you to extend the UML to fit your modeling needs more specifically. A stereotype is a UML modeling element that extends the existing elements. Stereotyping a UML element causes it to act as something else that has specific properties. A stereotype is represented as <<stereotype>> on the element being stereotyped.

A system is represented as a package with the stereotype of <<system>>, as seen in Figure 4-8. The system represents all the model elements that pertain to the particular project. You can also break a system into <<business systems>> and <<application systems>> when building more detailed models to make them smaller and more workable.

Figure 4-8 *System.*

A system usually is broken into multiple subsystems. Subsystems, like systems, are stereotyped packages with the stereotype of <<subsystem>>, as you can see in Figure 4-9. A subsystem is a grouping of model elements that are part of the overall system.

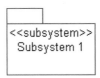

Figure 4-9 *Subsystem.*

Because a system or subsystem is a stereotyped package, it has all the properties and rules of a package. This means that model elements that are contained by the system and subsystem are owned by that package and can only be part of them and no other. The subsystem gives the project team an easy way to partition the system. Since a system contains multiple subsystems, everything contained within the subsystems is owned by the system that they roll up into. [SCOTT1] A diagram can display the logical architecture of a system (see Figure 4-10).

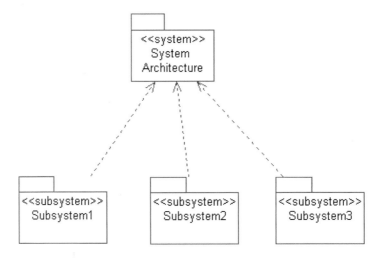

Figure 4-10 *System architecture.*

Physical Architecture

As stated earlier, architecture can be defined at both a logical and physical level. You will recall that the logical architecture is the more generic view of the architecture and how it works with less technical specificity.

The physical architecture, on the other hand, describes in more detail how the software and systems are designed, including specifics about how the architecture must fit into different technologies that exist within the organization and how the software integrates with itself and with other systems. We use several modeling elements and techniques to describe the physical architecture.

Operations

Operations specify the business logic concerning how a class functions and how classes can interact with each other. For example, getCustomer could be an operation on the Customer class. This provides the application logic for how to query for customer information (see Figure 4-11).

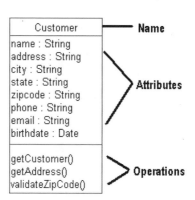

Figure 4-11   *Class with attributes and operations.*

Although all parts of the class can be translated to the physical code and become part of a running application, what causes the operations to differ is that they are much more specifically defined when you get into the physical implementation of the system and model. The operations are used in a logical architecture model to show expected software behavior but are more physically defined to show algorithms, functions, and more. They describe how the system will function and will be implemented with respect to the technology to be used.

We will revisit classes, attributes, operations, and so forth in Chapter 5 when we discuss application modeling.

Component Diagrams

Components are made up of one or more classes and describe parts of an application that can be assembled and reused. A component-based architecture (CBD) is the design of a software system made up of multiple components. For efficiency, it is important to develop software based on multiple smaller parts (components), which you can use to assemble the overall system. This enables you to reuse software components instead of writing them all from scratch.

Component-based architecture also enables different teams to work on the software and plug their pieces together using what are called "interfaces." An interface is a named set of operations that enable the components to work together through this interface code. Interfaces enable you to get and provide information to and from a component using code specific to the technology on which it is deployed. Figure 4-12 shows how a component and interface are displayed on a component diagram. The interface is displayed as a circle, but it can also be displayed as a typical class with the stereotype of <<interface>>. A component diagram can display multiple components and can show how those components integrate together, as seen in Figure 4-13.

Figure 4-12   *Component with interface.*

You can use a component diagram and components to model the architecture of different parts of your system. You can also use them to model the application internals, as we just discussed, as well as to view how different applications work together. For example, consider two executables (.exe), one that starts the other, both modeled as components. When writing Java applications, each Java file is represented in the UML as a component as well. This demonstrates that different levels of the architecture can be (and usually are) modeled as components. As classes represent the logical architecture of code, components represent the physical architecture and identify what has actually been implemented.

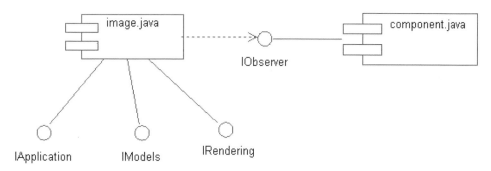

Figure 4-13 *Component diagram.*

Deployment Diagrams

Deployment diagrams represent the runtime architecture of your system. A deployment diagram can be made up of nodes that represent a piece of hardware that generally has memory and a processor built in. There are two different types of nodes: processor and device. Figure 4-14 shows what the deployment diagram elements look like.

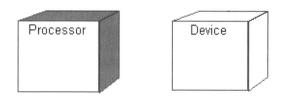

Figure 4-14 *Deployment diagram elements.*

Sometimes, a deployment diagram can show multiple applications running on a single device but on different processors. A server, for example, is a device that can have multiple processors running on it. A deployment diagram of a server would show that multiple applications could be running on a single server but on different processors.

When trying to understand the information architecture of your organization, it is important to know not only what software exists and how it is architected, but also how the architecture of the systems reside on the hardware. This means knowing what hardware exists, what software is on what hardware, what servers are used for backup, and how the software is stored on multiple pieces of hardware.

An enterprise architecture looks at the overall architecture and how all the pieces fit together. Many organizations, when defining their enterprise architectures, include not just hardware one would typically think of, such as servers, but also other pieces of hardware, such as aircraft, that are part of the enterprise. For instance, the DoDAF, which is used as the framework for the United States Department of Defense enterprise architecture, consists of visualizing the architecture of the different components that make up the information network, and they don't just include what you traditionally think of as software systems, but also airplanes, telecommunication systems, satellites, ships, and more because all these systems are run and managed by software, but often, one wouldn't consider such software in terms of applications. However, when the DoD defines their enterprise architecture, it is very important for them to understand where these applications fit in. Just as the military needs to understand how all facets of its air defense system work together, businesses need to understand how all of their systems work together.

Stereotypes

You can use stereotypes in all UML diagrams to better define the elements that you are modeling so that everyone who views the models understands what is being modeled and the story that is being told. Standard stereotypes are defined in the UML. We discussed some of them earlier in this chapter, and we will cover more later in this book. A stereotype can be just a title, but it can also carry a picture with it to better define itself and to provide an easy-to-understand graphical view the UML model. A few stereotypes we have seen used in deployment diagrams display the different types of deployment elements, such as different types of airplanes and ships (see Figure 4-15).

As discussed earlier, you also can use a deployment diagram in a more traditional sense: to understand the hardware and applications in your organization and how they exist within the enterprise. Figure 4-16 demonstrates how this can be achieved.

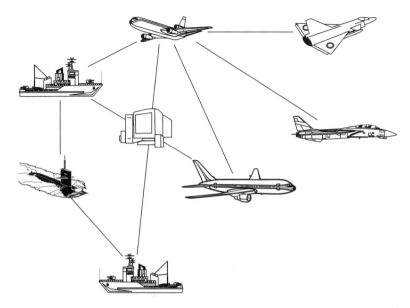

Figure 4-15 *Deployment diagram displaying pictures for stereotypes.*

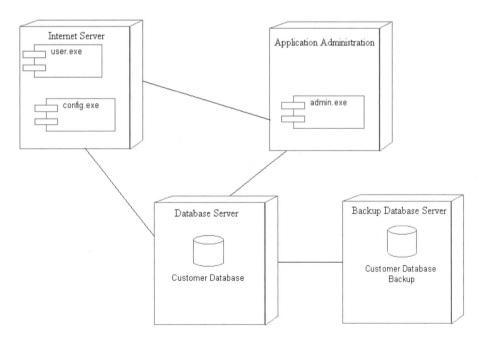

Figure 4-16 *Application deployment diagram.*

Architectural Patterns

The UML can also be used to depict architectural patterns. Patterns are repeatable architecture designs that have been tested and proven over time. Some people might say that *every* design has a pattern, similarly to saying every design has an architecture, but we are talking about patterns that are well-defined, tested, proven, and often used to improve designs and architectures. Patterns can be used for both logical and physical architectural designs.

Many well-known patterns are described in books that go into deep details on their usage. Some of the most popular patterns in the industry are known as the Gang of Four (GoF) patterns. These patterns were developed and made popular by four gentleman, Erich Gamma, Richard Helm, Ralph Johnson, and John Vlissides, in their book *Design Patterns: Elements of Reusable Object-Oriented Software*. The patterns described in that book are broken into different categories—Creational, Structural, and Behavioral. Figure 4-17 is a UML representation of one of the most popular GoF creational patterns called the *singleton*.

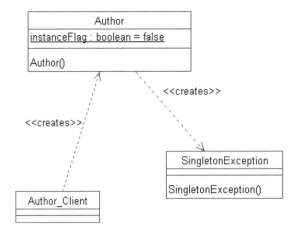

Figure 4-17   *Singleton pattern.*

The singleton pattern is applied against an individual class, and it creates several classes in a pattern. As you saw in Figure 4-17, the pattern is applied to a class named Author, and it creates two additional classes including some attributes and operations as part of the pattern. The intent of the singleton pattern is to ensure that a class only has one instance and to provide a global access point to it. [GAMM1] This pattern is quite logical in nature, but it can also be applied using additional methods with specific languages to become more physical.

There are also several patterns that are specifically physical in nature. An example of some physical patterns were created by a group of engineers at Sun Microsystems called the "Core J2EE Patterns" and are described in great detail in a book with the same title. Here, we will look at a pattern known as the Data Access Object (DAO) pattern.

An example DAO for a persistent object that represents Customer information is shown in Figure 4-18. The CustomerDAO creates a Customer value object. [ALUR1]

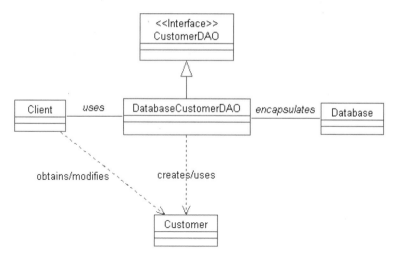

Figure 4-18 *DAO J2EE pattern.*

Although the DAO pattern might not be self-explanatory to a mere mortal, it is used in physical architectural design to provide database access in J2EE applications. Just like the logical architectural patterns, physical patterns are applied to existing classes and model elements to create additional elements using standard and proven processes.

What Is Model Driven Architecture?

Model Driven Architecture (MDA) is a term defined by the Object Modeling Group (OMG—www.omg.org) as an approach to system development that increases the power of models. By being model-driven, the approach provides a means for using models to direct the course of understanding, design, construction, deployment, operation, maintenance, and modification. [OMG1]

MDA isn't a new concept, but it is gaining more acceptance as the standards for defining architectures and developing applications become increasingly stable. Standards such as XML, CORBA, WSDL, XMI, and others provide a mechanism for approved ways of interchanging information between systems and software. When combining standards with tools for the creation of applications, you can create applications driven from architectures designed independently of the deployment technology.

By creating transformations between models in the UML and development technology languages, such as Java, C++, Visual Basic, and C#, and using the standard technologies to bridge the differences, you can create applications based on architectural designs. With technologies such as XML being used as a transformation language, you can model an architecture in the UML without concerning yourself with the deployment platform. Then, development can transform the designs created by architects into code. That code can and most likely will need to be customized at some point, but essentially the architectures that were designed are out of the way, ensuring that if a good architecture was defined, it will be implemented in the same way.

Deep Dive—Driving from Models

The most common way to achieve Model Driven Architecture (MDA) is by creating UML models of the logical application, generating first-cut code from those models, and then creating stub classes and some basic method code. The application at this point will need a lot of hand coding to create the business logic and tie the overall application together. This type of MDA is not what everyone would consider as the mission of MDA, but it is the most common and the most easily implemented for organizations that are not yet ready to bite off the entire vision. It ensures that architectures are designed prior to writing code, which helps to eliminate some poor designs but still puts the power of the application in the developer's hands.

Another way to implement MDA is by using a tool that enables you to model the overall application, including business logic, the base application, and the user interface, in a generic format, and then selecting a deployment platform to which it will generate. There are tools on the market today that can help you accomplish this tactic. They help organizations that do not have extensive technical knowledge but that need to generate applications using the latest technology. These tools raise the level of abstraction for the users so that you can model without a substantial knowledge of the deployment platform, and yet they enable you to build the application needed. When developing software using this type of tool, you can create a Java application the first time but then generate Visual Basic the second time because the level of abstraction is raised above deployment platforms.

These are two examples of ways to implement MDA, but they are the extremes. The first drives part of the application from the model, and the second drives the entire application from the model. You can achieve MDA using other methods that fall between these two extremes.

Although MDA is driven from a model and ends up with a running application, what sits between the model and application is what really drives the overall methodology: the standards. For example, having an XML model that is generic but mapped both to UML and the deployment environment enables the UML model to be transformed to XML and then transformed again to Visual Basic (for example), driving the full transformation from a generic model to a specific technology.

Topics to Consider

You may want to examine these additional topics:

- In the UML, there are less commonly used relationships. Explore the "realize" association.

- Frameworks are available that organizations have followed to build their application and enterprise architectures. These frameworks, such as Zachman, for example, provide best practices, standards, and guidance for building architectures.

- Investigate how you might do component modeling in additional detail to include the inner workings of the application and all the components needed.

Terms

Class	Attribute
Operation	Method
Interface	Association
Generalization	Dependency
Realization	Component
Device	Node
Processor	Stereotype
Framework	Architecture
Logical architecture	Physical architecture
Zachman	Model Driven Architecture

Summary

We began this chapter with a discussion of what an architecture is and how different organizations model architectures to understand both their software development assets and other non-software assets. The architecture can include hardware, processors within the hardware, and different components that make up an overall system.

Architectures can be logical and physical. A logical architecture looks at the architecture as it is and as it wants to be without looking at any specific technology, implementation, or physical attributes of the system. The physical architecture goes deep into how the architecture is implemented, looking at development languages, deployment platforms, physical hardware, and more. Understanding both types of architecture is important to achieve an understanding at all levels of the organization to ensure that you are doing what is right for the future.

Having a solid architecture when designing an application and system helps to ensure it can survive through time. As applications and systems evolve, they must be flexible so that you do not have to change the architecture or drastically change the application when the business changes. If systems aren't architected with this in mind, you might have to make significant changes or even rewrite the entire application just because some business processes have changed.

Review Questions

1. What elements are contained in the three compartments in a class?

2. Which of the following is not an architectural framework?

    a. Zachman Framework

    b. Federal Enterprise Architecture Framework

    c. Rational Architecture Framework

    d. Department of Defense Architecture Framework

3. True or False: Boolean is a standard UML attribute type that has two options, yes or no.

4. What geometric shape is used to visually describe an <<interface>>?

5. True or False: MDA stands for Model Driven Assets.

[ALUR1] Alur, Deepak, Dan Malks, and John Crupi. 2003. *Core J2EE Patterns, Second Edition: Best Practices and Design Strategies*. Upper Saddle River, NJ: Prentice Hall PTR.

[GAMM1] Gamma, Erich, Richard Helm, Ralph Johnson, and John Vlissides. 1995. *Design Patterns: Elements of Reusable Object-Oriented Software*. Reading, MA: Addison-Wesley.

[MEWE1] Merriam-Webster Online Dictionary. Available: *www.webster.com*.

[OMG1] Object Modeling Group. 2003. *MDA Guide*. Available: http://www.omg.org/docs/omg/03-06-01.pdf.

[SCOTT1] Kendall Scott. 2001. *UML Explained*. Boston, MA: Addison Wesley.

5

Application Modeling

Topics Covered in This Chapter

Why Should I Model My Applications?

> Our Second Response

> Behind the Question

Should I Model My Entire Application?

What About Programming Languages?

How Deeply Should I Model My Applications?

How Can the UML Model Applications?

> Review of Class Diagram Basics

>> Classes

>> Operations

>> Associations

>> Other Association Adornments

> More on Class Diagrams

>> Aggregation and Composition

>> Generalization

>> Association Classes

>> Constraints

> More on Sequence Diagrams

Topics to Consider

Terms

Summary

Review Questions

Why Should I Model My Applications?

You might be surprised that our first response to the question, "Why should I model my applications?" is that there are times when modeling applications is probably overkill. For instance, if the application is trivial, or if your development tools are powerful enough that you can "assemble" most of your application, or if your developers have developed similar applications and already know exactly how to implement the solution, modeling your application might be unnecessary.

However, for those of you who are building serious, business-critical applications, application modeling is necessary. In Chapter 2, "Business Models," we discussed some reasons for modeling your business, and many of those reasons apply to modeling applications. First, understanding what you already have is key, as most development efforts are not "greenfield" projects. Usually, some existing systems and software are in place that your team might not be familiar with and that needs to be interfaced to or modified. It's easier to understand existing applications through viewing a model than through tediously reading their code.

From the Real World—Tag! You're It (Again)!

We discussed a situation in Chapter 2 in which I inherited a critical application that had no documentation, that was missing some of the code and data files, and that no one understood (a situation in which many developers have found themselves). You might recall it took weeks to understand the application and longer to truly comprehend the underlying concepts and get the application up and running again. Also, additional time was lost and additional cost incurred when dealing with new users who did not understand how or why the application operated as it did. If there had been a model of this application, most of these problems and their corresponding costs would have been avoided.

But let us continue with the rest of the story. After a series of "renovations" of this application, it was in very good shape, everything was operational, and all the pieces were accounted for and were under version control. There was even a preliminary set of documentation. Everything was on track. However, there was no model of this application (my organization did not do application modeling).

There were a few minor, non-critical defects that needed to be ferreted out, but they didn't impede operation and wouldn't prohibit delivery. What a great time to take some vacation. So I did. I came back refreshed and ready to continue with the renovation of this application. As I worked, I noted some odd behaviors that I had not seen before. The application still operated well enough, but it was doing things that it should not have been doing, such as sending duplicate messages to the operator. Were these intentional (resulting from some distant corner of the application I hadn't examined) or were they a defect? The application certainly hadn't been behaving like this before I left.

After a few days of digging through the code, I found that the code was different. A few subtle changes had been made. More investigation revealed that one of the new users had raised a concern about the application's operation to my manager. For some reason, the boss decided to "fix" the code without telling anyone. Yes, he did change the application's behavior to satisfy this one user. In the process, he introduced a handful of new, real defects. He might have been able to make a correct change if we had a model of the software, but like many programmers who inherit software, he did not have a model. He did a quick assessment of the code and made the changes, "fixing" the "problem" without understanding the side effects (defects) he was causing.

Lessons Learned

1. Models of your applications, especially the more intricate or critical applications, require time to create, but they can save much more time when changes need to be made to your software.

2. When you go on vacation, lock up your code. Configuration management is critical for successful development.

Another reason you should model your applications is because when you are designing new applications, changes often occur *during* your design phase. Having a model makes it much easier to assess the impact of changes that might be made because you can *see* the parts of the application that will be impacted. As indicated in the sidebar "From the Real World—Tag! You're It (Again)!," when code needs to be changed, the design models can be examined to see if the proposed changes might break the application elsewhere.

A visual model of your application also makes it much easier for you to determine whether your design is meeting the needs of the business. You can literally point to the element that is satisfying a requirement instead of pointing to a stack of textual specifications.

Lastly, as we said earlier, a model provides a "point-of-focus" to enable your stakeholders to discuss and resolve design issues. As the former United States President Dwight Eisenhower said, "Plans are nothing; planning is everything." It's not just the models themselves; it's the process and thinking that you must go through to create the models that provide tremendous value. Modeling forces you to think, and by thinking it through, you will create better designs.

Our Second Response

Our second response to those who ask why they should model their applications is quite simple: You already model anyway. You just don't call it modeling.

Remember the definitions of a model in Chapter 1, "Introduction to the UML"—a model is a representation of something not yet built. Walk around the cubicles in most software development departments and look at the whiteboards. You will find all manner of models scrawled upon them: block diagrams that model the structure of programs and their subroutines, flowcharts modeling the control flow of programs, long partitioned rectangles modeling record structures, a network of interconnected squares modeling the linkages on a web site, and yes, even some UML diagrams. These are all examples of modeling. Modeling is simply a technique used as part of the analysis and design of software and systems, and many of you are already doing it, just not in a formalized way. UML merely brings a formal approach, symbology, and meaning to your modeling activities.

Behind the Question

Often, there are really other questions (or fears) behind the "why model applications" question. Most people who ask why they should model applications already understand why they should. What they are really asking is related to other factors. Managers, for instance, often ask this question because they are really concerned about the time it takes to model. They do not realize that the reason coding takes up the majority of effort in a development project can often be attributed to incomplete design. The job of resolving the design details is passed down the line and left to the programmers to perform while they are writing code. Management does not see this "hidden design" because it is embedded within the coding efforts. As we said earlier, you really *are* doing modeling (i.e., design); you just call it something else.

Other managers only measure progress by counting how many lines of code have been written. These people usually come from the "Ready-Set-Code!" school of software development. This is an unfortunate (and prevalent) mentality in our industry. If this describes you, you also need to think about the larger issues: meeting the business's needs, producing a resilient design, creating a high-quality product, and the various other benefits of modeling cited in this and earlier chapters.

Cost is also behind the question of whether to model. The cost is not really in the modeling itself (as discussed earlier in this chapter, you *will* do this work eventually, whether formally modeling or not). The real cost is the up front investment in skilled people or in training your existing staff to learn to model properly. However, this "one time" cost is recovered in every subsequent project you do, primarily through reduced rework and defect removal costs (recall the chart in Figure 3-1). The focus should be on creating an application that works as intended (otherwise, if it does not do what your customer wants, *all* your time and money has been wasted) and the total lifecycle cost of the application. Anyway, as a manager, isn't staff development part of your job?

Similarly, if you are a programmer asking this question, and none of the previous discussion moves you, we would ask why you wouldn't want to learn a new skill? After all, a programmer's employability rests on his skills. Also, do you really want to be just a coder? Or do you want to earn that "software engineer" title? Are you satisfied with hammering nails? Or do you want to be the architect of that cathedral? UML isn't going away. You should add it to your skill set.

Should I Model My Entire Application?

Whenever possible, you should model your entire application (or system). That way, you have conscious control over the architecture and design of the application. In some cases—for instance, when you don't have control over the entire system—you can't model it in its entirety. Still, it can be very valuable to model what you do have control over.

From the Real World—More Holes than Swiss Cheese

While working as a systems integrator on a very large project (thus not having direct control over any particular implementation piece of the project), I was looking at a product production scenario that others had specified in the system requirements. The scenario was quite complex. I was just getting to know object-oriented techniques at that time, and I decided to develop a statechart diagram of that scenario. (As you will learn in an upcoming chapter, statechart diagrams typically depict the state of a specific object. I decided to try this technique on an entire scenario.)

To my great surprise, I found there were a number of holes in this production scenario. In many situations, this scenario did not specify what should happen under certain common conditions. In other words, if this scenario were implemented, it would fail miserably. I did not "own" this part of the system, but I was still able to learn about it and find the flaws in it through modeling, which enabled me to recommend key changes.

Lessons Learned

1. Don't be afraid to use modeling techniques in creative ways (e.g., using the statechart diagram against a scenario instead of an object). As long as you use them properly (i.e., don't undermine the principles underlying the diagram or technique), you might find new ways to extract great value from them. The UML police will not come and kick your door in for doing so.

If you are dealing with an existing system (maybe you have to interface with this system or need to refurbish or replace a part of it while keeping it operational), you might just choose to "wrap" that existing system. When you wrap an existing system, you "surround" it with an interface layer that presents the same, existing interfaces to external applications but that enables the underlying technology to change. When modeling, you would just model the interfaces to the system or application, not the internals (later in this chapter, when discussing classes, we will revisit modeling interfaces). This also would enable you to add new interfaces without disrupting the existing ones (indeed, your new interfaces might use the old interfaces, but this would all be hidden under the wrapper), and it would enable you to change the underlying implementation while keeping the interface the same.

In cases where you are limited by budgetary, schedule, or staff skill issues (i.e., you don't have many people who can do the modeling), you should model only the critical parts of the system. For example, you might choose to model in detail only your high-priority use cases. Any part of the application or system that is high-risk should be modeled. If your application is a real-time application, it should be modeled. They are too critical to risk development based on poor, unidentified designs. After all, if you can't make these critical pieces work, why bother with the less critical parts?

What About Programming Languages?

Programming languages have made significant advances, adding reusable component libraries, powerful programming frameworks, and so forth. However, just because a language is labeled as an "object-oriented" language does not mean it can substitute for good object-oriented analysis and design.

A programming language, even though it might provide architectural components for you to work with, cannot ensure good design and cannot ensure that your application will meet your customer's needs. That's like saying that just because a manufacturer can obtain a full pre-assembled wheel assembly and use it in its mini-vans, the final vehicle will meet stability standards and will handle well. Languages and tools cannot substitute for proper analysis and design.

How Deeply Should I Model My Applications?

Often, people who are ready to model their applications ask when they should move from modeling activities into implementation, or how much detail their models should contain. In certain situations, putting as much detail as possible into your models is in your best interest—for instance, when you are modeling something that is critical and/or high-risk, such as an implanted medical device (in which case lives are at stake), or when there will be huge financial implications if your system fails. Such dire consequences justify that you model your applications as deeply as possible.

Situations in which performance or reliability are critical are also good candidates, as are situations in which you are outsourcing development. What do these situations have in common? These are cases in which you want to limit design tradeoffs by fully defining (i.e., modeling) your application. You do not want to leave key design decisions that could impact your critical factors, such as performance or security, to a junior programmer. For example, that junior programmer might choose to implement the code in a manner that reduces memory consumption. Although this seems harmless, memory utilization might not be an issue for you—you might need a system that has superlative performance. You don't want to defer such critical design tradeoffs to implementation. You should fully model such critical systems in detail so that you get what you really need.

In non-critical situations, the amount of detail you put into your models is often governed by your project schedule, budget, and the skill of your staff. Although including more detail is generally better, often you will have to pragmatically balance all these factors. One indicator you might watch is rate of change. If the details in your model are in a constant state of flux, such as if the operations specified are changing frequently, it might be too soon to hand off your models to development for implementation because the design is obviously immature. You should wait until some reasonable level of stability sets in (because change never stops) before you proceed. The definition of "reasonable" is different for each organization, of course. However, when your rate of change levels off at some low, stable level, you probably are ready to begin to implement your design models.

How Can the UML Model Applications?

Your business models have established why you are building this system (i.e., how it will support the business). Your use case models have depicted how the actors will use the system. And the architecture models set the initial organization of your system. Armed with this understanding, you are well prepared to model your application. These prior models limit the "shape" of the application. The business and use case models serve to limit the design space (which is a good thing because it takes the whole universe of possible solutions and constrains that solution space). The architecture models set the overall structure of your solution. In this way, developing these models helps to control the cost and schedule of the project.

Review of Class Diagram Basics

After these boundaries are set, the most common diagram utilized to depict the static structure of your application is the class diagram. Class diagrams were introduced earlier in Chapter 4, "Architectural Modeling." There, you saw class diagrams used for architectural modeling. In case you skipped past that section, let's review some of the class diagram basics as they pertain to application modeling and then explore some additional modeling elements you might find in these diagrams.

Classes

The class diagram shows the important classes in the application and their relationships to the other classes. Classes primarily represent the "things" in the system. Through the development of the upstream models (business, requirements, architecture), you will have already discovered many important classes. Finding these classes is much harder to do well without these other models, but it can be done. If you don't have the upstream models, just look at the problem statement for your application. Pick out the real "things" in the problem statement, such as account, aircraft, customer, product, transmitter, report, and so forth (see Figure 5-1). These will be the *domain classes* that should be in your class diagrams. As the models develop, non-real things will show up as classes, too, such as controller classes that coordinate processing, among others.

Figure 5-1 *A class representing a planet.*

But what are classes with regard to implementation of your software? Classes describe a group of similar *objects*. Classes are templates used to create those objects in your application.

Watch Out—Breaking the Rules

The terms "class" and "object" are often used interchangeably when discussing UML models. Although this is technically incorrect, as long as you keep in mind that the class is the specification and the object(s) are the implementation, you should be fine. Don't worry, we won't tell the "Grand High Poobahs of Modeling" what you've done.

Just as a cookie cutter will cut out many identical cookies, if you have a class "Planet," you can create multiple planet *objects* in your application by using the Planet class. Now, having a bunch of similar planets might not be very interesting. But just as you can take many of the same cookies and vary them by adding sprinkles or icing or food coloring, you can specialize your classes through *polymorphism* (more on this later in this chapter).

You will need to capture important information about your classes. You do this by using attributes (similar to the descriptions in Chapter 4 around architecture, but now specific for the application's design itself). Attributes capture the essential characteristics of the class that are needed by the application—not *all* its characteristics, just those that are applicable to the problem at hand. For example, if your application simulates the position of the planets in the solar system, your Planet class might capture the planet's distance from the sun and orbit (see Figure 5-2) but would not capture the core composition of the planet.

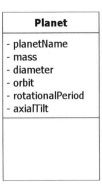

Figure 5-2   *Planet class with attributes.*

Watch Out—Dear Occupant

The attributes you capture in your classes determine the nature of the abstraction that the class is trying to capture. This can be critical to the success of your project. I was involved in a post-mortem on a project that had "serious difficulties." One problem centered on the class "Address." This team's concept of "address" was that an address was the location of your home. Although this is not an incorrect abstraction of address, it was not the best for this application. The application was not managing the location of homes. This was a mailing application. In this context, the better abstraction for address was that it is where you send mail (which might be your home, a hotel if you are traveling, a hospital if you are ill, a vacation home, etc.).

Lessons Learned

1. Make sure your classes and their attributes are capturing the right abstraction for your application.

Another way of considering attributes is in the context of data. Object-oriented analysis and design *encapsulates* data and processing together. Your attributes are the data that is encapsulated inside the class. The data (attributes) inside the class can be available to other classes depending on the attribute's visibility. Attributes can have public, protected, private, or package visibility (see Table 5-1).

Table 5-1 *Kinds of Visibility*

Visibility	Symbol	Meaning
Private	-	Only the class itself can access these attributes.
Protected	#	Any child class of this class can access these attributes.
Public	+	Any class can access these attributes.
Package	~	Any class in the same package can access these attributes.

In theory, a class's attributes should all be private to ensure strong encapsulation (this protects the attributes from being accessed or altered by other objects, except as allowed by the owning object). However, you might find situations, say, during detailed design or implementation, where the level of encapsulation needs to be "softened." In these cases, you can use the other levels of visibility to allow greater accessibility to a class's attributes. However, attributes should remain private unless there is a strong need otherwise.

So what can classes do? That is established by the class's operations.

Operations

Operations are the services that the class provides. Operations are shown in the third compartment of the class symbol. Typically, a class will contain the operations that provide access to its attributes along with the other processing functions of the class (see Figure 5-3). This is how external objects get access to the private attributes of the owning object. The class itself might not perform all of the operations within it, but the class is responsible for ensuring that *something* performs the operations (such as another object that is the one actually doing the work). In this case, the class is acting as a controller class, controlling all or part of the application.

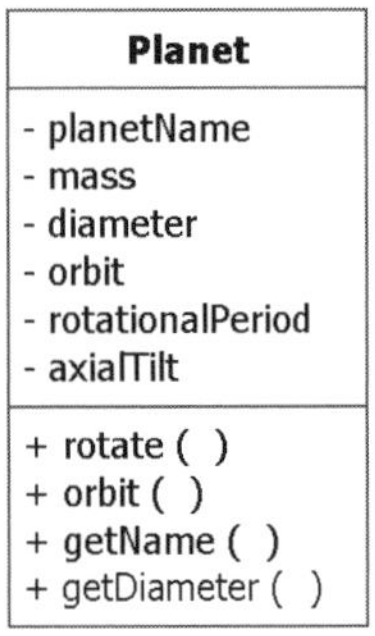

Planet
- planetName
- mass
- diameter
- orbit
- rotationalPeriod
- axialTilt
+ rotate ( )
+ orbit ( )
+ getName ( )
+ getDiameter ( )

Figure 5-3   *Planet class with operations added.*

Depending on the maturity of the diagram you have, just the operation name might be shown. As an operation develops, its full *signature* will develop, showing its name, parameters, default values, return type, and so forth (see Figure 5-4). How much detail is actually specified will depend on how your organization uses modeling, that is, how much detail you require before handing the design to the programmers for implementation.

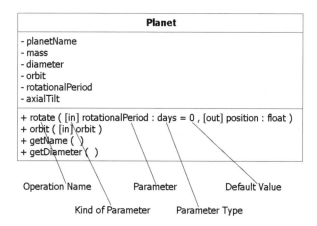

Figure 5-4 *Planet class with operation signature.*

Watch Out—Breaking the Rules II

Similarly to how people use the terms "class" and "object" interchangeably when discussing UML models (discussed earlier in this chapter), you will hear people interchange the terms "operation" and "method." This, too, is technically incorrect. Although an operation specifies a service provided by its class, a method is the implementation of that operation. Various possible methods (implementations) can satisfy an operation. For example, if you have a Sort operation, the method could implement it with a bubble sort, a hash sort, or some other sorting algorithm.

You might also encounter operations that are marked "{abstract}". This indicates that this class doesn't implement the operation. The operation will be implemented in a child class where you will see that same operation in the child's operation compartment. This is one way to have specific implementations of an operation. For example, the operation "load" would be implemented very differently in a "Rifle" class than in a "Blowgun" class. This is the central idea of the concept of *polymorphism* (see Figure 5-5): If the child specifies an operation that is also specified in the parent class, the child's operation will *override* the parent's operation. In this manner, the parent's behavior can be refined or replaced by the child's functionality.

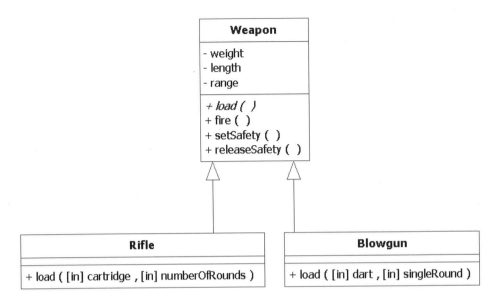

Figure 5-5   *Polymorphism.*

A class's operations can be functions that the class executes of its own voli-tion or functions that other objects request the class to execute. The opera-tions that others can request of a class can be affected by visibility (refer to Table 5-1), which applies to operations as well as attributes.

Another UML element that can restrict what services other classes can request of a class is the *interface*. An interface is merely a group of operations an external element can see and thus request (see Figure 5-6). The class designer determines which operations are revealed by an interface.

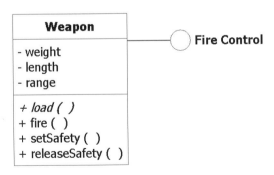

Figure 5-6   *Class with an interface.*

Associations

As discussed in Chapter 4, associations show the relationships between the objects in your system. They typically show the communication pathways between the objects, which can be bidirectional or unidirectional, as discussed earlier. Directionality (a.k.a. navigability) usually should be specified later in the design phase when you have more knowledge of how the processing will actually be traversing the associations. In this way, you will know how the implementation of the associations should be optimized.

Other Association Adornments

Some of the adornments that appear on association ends (e.g., multiplicity, diamonds) were also discussed in Chapter 4. You will often run into a few others.

Rolenames can appear on the end of an association. These rolenames describe the class that is attached to that same end of the association as the rolename. The function of the rolename is to indicate how the class will behave in that specific relationship with the class it is associated with. This is similar to the various roles we all play in life. When I am serving as an engineer, I perform certain behaviors. When I am acting as an investor, I perform different behaviors (although there can be some common behaviors). An engineer might read, analyze, design, build, etc. An investor might read, analyze, buy, sell, manage an account, etc. (see Figure 5-7). In this way, rolenames partition the behaviors of their classes.

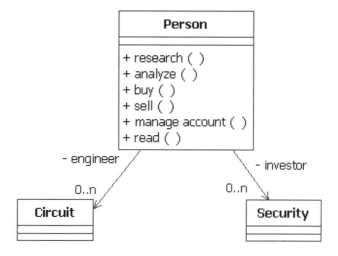

Figure 5-7 *Rolenames.*

Although rolenames partition the behavior(s) a class presents in an association with another class, *qualifiers* partition the set of objects that can participate in an association. Let's look at some examples using the classes Payroll and Person.

Figure 5-8 says that the Payroll department pays a Person. Figure 5-9 shows how a rolename can be added for clarity—Payroll is paying a Person who is acting as an employee (not a contractor or vendor). Yet, in both of these diagrams, there is little specificity.

Figure 5-8   *Unadorned association.*

Figure 5-9   *Association with rolename.*

When we add a qualifier (employee number), as in Figure 5-10, we now know that only that specific Person object participates in the association (i.e., only that Person with a specific employee number is being paid). If you augment this with multiplicity, you add more information to the model. In Figure 5-11, we see that because of the 0..1 multiplicity, Payroll pays either nobody (indicating an employee number that is not assigned to an employee) or one specific employee.

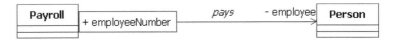

Figure 5-10   *Association with rolename and qualifier.*

Figure 5-11   *Association with rolename, qualifier, and multiplicity.*

Change the qualifier and multiplicity, and you get new semantics, as in Figure 5-12, where Payroll pays many full-time employees (the part-time employees are excluded by the qualifier "full-time").

Figure 5-12   *Association with rolename and qualifier selecting a set of objects.*

More on Class Diagrams

Aggregation and Composition

In Chapter 4, two related association types were mentioned—*aggregation* and *composition.* (In UML 2.0, a composition association is also called a composite aggregation.) Figure 5-13 shows both associations.

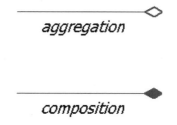

Figure 5-13   *Aggregation and composition associations.*

Aggregation is shown with an empty (or hollow) diamond, whereas composition is noted with a filled-in diamond. In both cases, the diamond appears on the "Whole" end of the association. These associations are read: "The Part is part of the Whole" and "The Whole has a Part" (the number of specific parts is determined by the multiplicity on the part end of the association).

These associations carry the special meaning that one element of the association "is part of" the other. The difference between aggregation and composition is how tight the relationship is between the participating elements. Aggregation is a looser form of association, whereas composition indicates a much tighter form of containment. In a composition, the Part(s) can only be part of *one* Whole. Also, with composition, when the Whole is destroyed, so are all its parts. (In fact, it is the responsibility of the Whole to ensure that its parts are destroyed.) In Figure 5-14, you can see such relationships as they pertain to a flashlight.

Figure 5-14 *Aggregation and composition of a flashlight.*

A flashlight has a switch. This is a composition because the switch is part of that one flashlight—When you throw away (destroy) the flashlight, the switch goes with it. On the other hand, you could remove the battery from the flashlight and use it in another one, which is why this association is shown as an aggregation.

One caveat—these "part of" relationships aren't just for *physical* elements. For example, a Person can have a Belief, or a BrandName can have Market-Value.

Generalization

You have seen the generalization relationship earlier in this chapter (refer to Figure 5-5). The class at the arrowhead end of the association is the super-class. The class or classes at the non-arrowhead end of this association are the subclasses. The superclass-subclass relationship is similar to a parent-child relationship. The children (subclasses) *inherit* attributes, operations, and relationships from the parent (superclass). Figure 5-15 shows such a relationship. The parent (Weapon) has the attributes weight, length, and range. Through *inheritance*, the children (Rifle and Blowgun) inherit these attributes; that is, they also have weight, length, and range, even though they might not be explicitly shown in these subclasses. The same holds true for the operations—the children inherit them from the parent. In this particular case, as discussed earlier, the operation "load" is overridden (i.e., redefined) by the children.

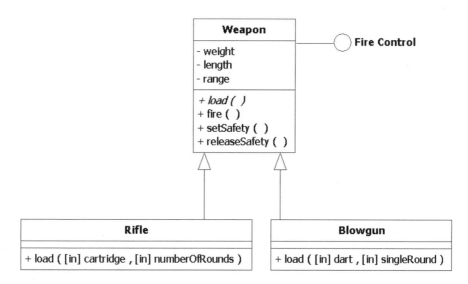

Figure 5-15   *Generalization.*

Association Classes

Sometimes, as you start to connect all these classes (through associations), you might run across situations where the important concept is not the classes themselves but the relationship between the classes. For example, Figure 5-16 shows an investor who invests in various securities.

Figure 5-16   *Basic association.*

If your application is required to calculate the tax implications of the investments, it will need to understand things like when the security was bought and sold, the respective prices, and so forth. So, is the purchase date an attribute of the investor? Obviously not. The security? Not really—the purchase date is not an intrinsic property of the security. This kind of information is descriptive of the *relationship* between the investor and security, not the classes. It is the *relationship* between the two that is the key concept in this situation.

So, where is this information captured? In an *association class*. (Just when you thought it was safe, when you thought you had this class and association stuff understood, here comes a curve ball.) Association classes are associations that have some of the characteristics of classes. In this example, the critical information that is needed revolves around the *ownership* of the security by the investor (see Figure 5-17).

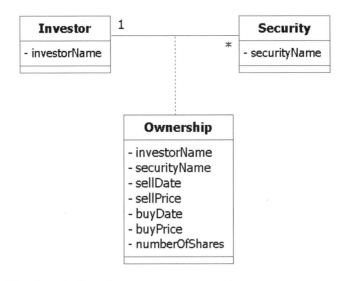

Figure 5-17   *Association class.*

The association class Ownership holds the important information about the *relationship* between the other two classes. (Also, you will often see association classes on many-to-many associations.) Without the investor, there will be no purchase. Without the security, there is nothing to buy. You need both the investor and the security together. The relationship, and thus the association class, cannot exist unless both of the associated classes exist.

Constraints

To add even more meaning and expressiveness to your designs, UML provides *constraints*. Constraints are annotations that add additional restrictions or specificity to model elements. Figure 5-18 revisits our payroll example. If the pay period for the company is every week, a constraint can be added to make that explicit (shown between the curly braces).

Constraints can be timing constraints, order constraints, uniqueness, or whatever you need for your situation.

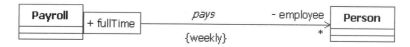

Figure 5-18   *Constraint.*

More on Sequence Diagrams

Just as the class diagrams depict the static structure of your application, sequence diagrams can depict the dynamic behavioral aspects of your application. As discussed in Chapters 2 and 3, they show how the objects of your application collaborate by using messages to achieve a desired outcome. The use of these diagrams for yet another purpose (i.e., application modeling) is additional testimony to their versatility. Another behavioral diagram, the statechart diagram, will be discussed in Chapter 8.

The following diagrams show an example of the use of sequence diagrams in application modeling. For context, Figure 5-19 shows a use case diagram for a regulatory compliance subsystem of a medical records management system.

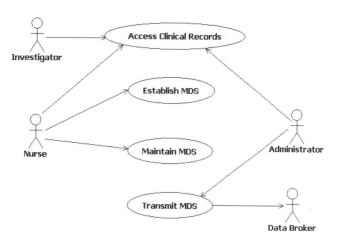

Figure 5-19   *Compliance use case diagram.*

Here, we will focus on the Transmit MDS use case. To meet regulatory requirements, the healthcare facility must transmit to the government information on the patients in their care. This set of medical records is called a Minimum Data Set (MDS). The sequence diagram captures the dynamic behavior of the system (see Figure 5-20).

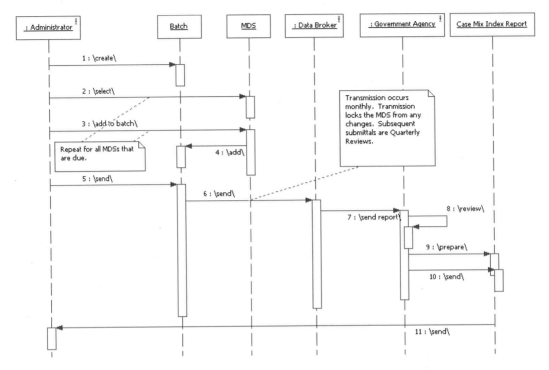

Figure 5-20 *Compliance sequence diagram.*

You can see by following the message flow in this diagram how the Administrator creates a "Batch" of MDSs to be transmitted. MDSs are selected and added to the Batch. The Batch is then sent to the Data Broker and so forth as the sequence continues.

This sequence diagram shows the dynamic interactions between the things in the system. This provides the basis for establishing the structure of these elements, which is captured in Figure 5-21—the class diagram for the Transmit MDS use case.

Designing systems in an object-oriented fashion is quite iterative. As this class design was being developed, the designer realized a new system element was needed to manage the creation and transmission of the Batches. Thus, you see a Batch Controller was added to the class diagram. In a rigorous process, the sequence diagram would be updated to include the Batch Controller. Iteration and changes between the various diagrams is quite common as application design progresses. (If you are interested in understanding the process and development of this example, from business modeling through application and database design, see our book *UML for Database Design* [NAIB3], where this case study is developed in detail.)

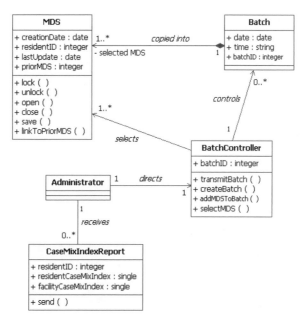

Figure 5-21   *Compliance class diagram.*

Topics to Consider

You might want to examine these additional topics:

- Classes can have additional compartments beyond the name, attribute, and operation compartments. Find examples of how these are used.
- Examine the often-used concept of *derived attributes*.
- Explore the *dependency* relationship.
- Investigate the difference between implementation classes, types, and parameterized classes (a.k.a. template classes).

- The associations in this chapter have been between two classes. There are situations where more than two classes are part of a single relationship. Investigate these "n-ary associations."
- Compare and contrast sequence diagrams and collaboration diagrams.

Terms

Interface	Wrap
Class	Object
Polymorphism	Abstraction
UML police	Encapsulation
Visibility	Operation
Signature	Abstract
Override	Association
Adornment	Rolename
Qualifier	Multiplicity
Aggregation	Composition
Containment	Association class
Constraints	Attribute
Generalization	Inheritance

Summary

This chapter's discussion started with reasons for modeling your applications. We pointed out that the average software system designer already models applications in the form of block diagrams, flowcharts, and so forth. You learned how modeling more formally (with UML) offers benefits both for applications that are new or legacy, especially where the software is critical, complex, and/or changing. We also examined the personal and career-related reasons for modeling your applications.

Then we examined the question of the breadth and depth to which you should model applications. Although modeling the complete application is the best case, you learned of various criteria and approaches for modeling selective areas of your application or system. You also learned that you should not believe that programming languages can substitute for proper analysis and design.

Finally, you learned the main elements found in class diagrams: classes with their attributes and operations, and associations between classes. You were introduced to the concepts of polymorphism, encapsulation, visibility, and constraints. You learned how the rolenames, qualifiers, and multiplicity adornments can be used. We also contrasted two special associations: aggregation and composition. Finally, generalization and inheritance were also discussed.

Review Questions

1. True or False: Polymorphism is the concept that states a class's data is hidden from outside entities and can only be accessed by external entities through the operations provided by that class.

2. What restriction does a rolename apply to a class?

3. A qualifier selects specific object instances of the class:
   a. On the end of the association nearest to the qualifier
   b. On the far end of the association

4. True or False: In an aggregation, when the "whole" is destroyed, all the parts are not necessarily destroyed.

5. Which of the following are not a type of visibility:
   a. Private
   b. Partial
   c. Virtual
   d. Public
   e. Abstract
   f. Package
   g. Protected

[NAIB3] Naiburg, Eric J. and Robert A. Maksimchuk. 2001. *UML for Database Design*. Boston, MA: Addison-Wesley.

6

Database Modeling

Topics Covered in This Chapter

UML for Database Design?

    The Fallacy About Notations

How Can I Leverage UML Models Created by Others?

    Use Case Models

    Activity Models

    Class Models

What Types of Database Models Can Be Created Using the UML?

    Conceptual Models

    Logical Models

    Physical Models

Topics to Consider

Terms

Summary

Review Questions

UML for Database Design?

Yes, database design can be accomplished using the UML. The UML itself was originally created with an understanding of traditional database modeling. The UML's creators indicate that they consider UML to be a superset of database design methods. Formalized modeling of databases has been widely accepted for years, while application modeling in general is still not as widely followed formally by organizations. It is often thought of as an activity only done formally when describing complicated application architectures. The creators of the UML were able to leverage work that had been done in the past to create the database design standards and that had wide acceptance by the industry to help them drive their creation of the UML.

Not only can you build conceptual, logical, and physical database models using the UML, but you can also bring teams together by sharing a common approach and language. One of the most common causes of application failure is poor communication. If you can have the database designers, application developers, and others working together to design a complete solution, your odds of success increase. A database designer might not build all the UML diagrams that we have discussed in the previous chapters, but he can leverage them to ensure that everyone is following, understanding, and working with the same set of requirements, business processes, assumptions, and decisions. This increases the team's efficiency.

So, does this alone mean that the UML can support database design? No, this information alone does not mean the UML can support database design, but as we continue throughout this chapter, you will come to understand that **yes**, UML can be and is used for database design. Although we will cover some of the basics for using UML to design databases, we will not go into the depth needed to fully complete the task. For more discussion and much deeper detail on using the UML for designing databases, take a look at our book *UML for Database Design* (ISBN: 0-201-72163-5).

The Fallacy About Notations

We have spent a lot of time traveling the world, talking about the UML and how it applies to database design. These meetings, presentations, and discussions always start with an explanation that the UML is a language that includes a notation that can be adapted for most types of modeling, including database design. The first ten minutes are spent providing an understanding of how UML can support database design just like any other notation.

IDEF1X (Integration Definition for Information Modeling) is a well-known database design notation that was originally developed for the U.S. Federal Government and subsequently was adopted as an industry standard. IE (Information Engineering), also known as crows feet notation, is probably the most widely used notation.

It doesn't really matter what notation you use; the end result is going to be the same—a good design should result in a high-quality database. In the same light, any notation used in creation of a poor design will create a low-quality database. What is most important is that you can enforce and communicate your designs using the notation you choose. In Figures 6-1, 6-2, and 6-3, you can see how different notations show exactly the same thing. They may look a little different, but they express the same concept.

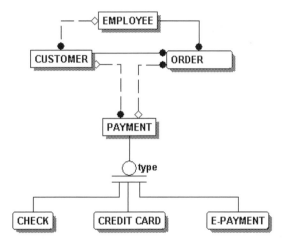

Figure 6-1   *IDEF1X.*

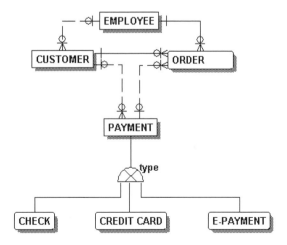

Figure 6-2   *Information engineering.*

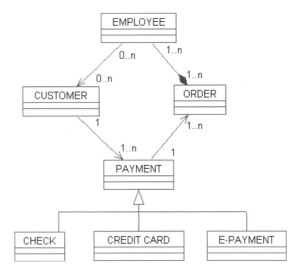

Figure 6-3 *UML.*

A major advantage you gain with using UML for designing databases is that model reviewers, even those with limited technical knowledge such as line of business owners, find it easier to read than other languages. For example, because UML spells out the *cardinality* (also known as *multiplicity*, represented by the little numbers on the association lines) directly on the relationship, you do not have to infer what the different types of line markings mean. You just read the relationship.

It's fallacious to assume that UML cannot be used to model databases. The previous examples refer to a logical data model, but the same thing can be done in exactly the same way for physical data models. As the chapter continues, we will demonstrate the use of UML for conceptual, logical, and physical data modeling.

How Can I Leverage UML Models Created by Others?

Database designers can take advantage of the benefits of UML, even if they are using something else to model their databases, because they can draw on the models created by others on the development team to understand the overall system that is being built.

UML models that you have seen previously in this book (and will continue to see through to the end) describe the things needed to build a well-architected system. The database designers can jump-start their database designs and ensure a common understanding amongst the team by taking advantage of other team members' work with the UML.

From the Real World—Taking Off with a Common Understanding

A large airline organization needed to ensure that the people building their systems all were on the same page. They had business analysts gathering information about the business and modeling it. They had architects building application designs, developers acting on the designs by writing software, data analysts designing the logical and first cut physical database designs, and database administrators realizing the database design in code. However, each team had a different manager, and they weren't communicating with each other regarding what their teams were doing. This often resulted in architectures that had to be reworked late in the game. They first realized the problem when they were trying to integrate systems but were using different terms in different ways, including calling entities one thing in the database and something different in the application code.

My first visit proved to be quite interesting. This multi-billion dollar airline was building software to run their business and was beginning to figure out the best way to communicate across teams involved in the software and system creation process. They recognized that the problems they were having stemmed very much from a lack of communication— not in terms of talking, but in terms of failing to work together to create the designs. They decided to combine the organizations and create a group that reported to the same management structure. They felt that by ensuring that all the teams were under the same management, the teams would be much more likely to work together.

Next, they formed teams that included all the stakeholders in a project to work through the initial requirements together. Don't take this the wrong way. There weren't 50 people on these teams. Each group had representation so that the business, development, architecture, and data teams were all now working together in small, manageable teams that could work effectively with five or six people.

continues

From the Real World—Taking Off with a Common Understanding (*continued*)

These teams were responsible for creating the system requirements, including a common dictionary they called their conceptual data dictionary. They used the UML to define much of the work they were doing together so that everyone had a common language with which to communicate. The data analysts still used one of the non-UML notations for building the data models, but they all shared the rest in common. They really started to see the value when newer systems were being brought online and they didn't have to worry if in one system "agent" meant travel agent and in another it meant gate agent. Because they were working against a common set of requirements and using these common models to share information about the architecture, the teams knew that there were many types of agents, and if they were to use one in a design, they knew its meaning.

This was the first time in a long time that I saw database teams working together with others to design a common architecture for an organization. They brought the different groups together to create a team that could understand the business' intentions to avoid conflicting solutions within the project.

Lessons Learned

1. Common language leads to common understanding.

2. Sometimes, even though you are working toward a common goal, if the organizations trying to achieve it are different, the organizations' structure can get in the way.

3. When building a system, working together as a cross-functional team greatly increases the possibilities of success because you're sharing information and, maybe even more importantly, you're resolving the problems together.

We are not going to rehash all that you have read in the previous chapters about the different types of models. Instead, we'll provide some additional insight on how the models can be leveraged in your database designs.

Use Case Models

To start with, many organizations take advantage of use cases and actors as discussed in Chapter 2, "Business Models." Use cases describe how the system will work, and actors are used to model people and systems that interact with the use cases. In this chapter, we will focus on these elements as they are used in the creation of database designs. Use case and business use case models can be very valuable to the data architects (database designers) to understand more about the data that will need to be captured and how they might optimize it based on who will access it and how.

As a designer of the database, you can get your first look into the initial components of a conceptual data model by using use cases. Even at this early point, you can see from the business use case model in Figure 6-4 that things such as Clinical Records, Residents, Physicians, and Accountants are important parts of the system. Based on this information, you can determine which things are needed in the logical data model when you are ready to design at the logical level.

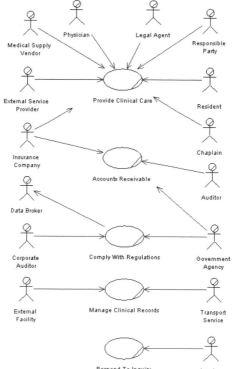

Figure 6-4   *The Provide Resident Care business use case model.*

Some access and processing information is also available—from the diagram, it's clear that the External Facility and Transport Service have access to the Clinical Records. [NAIB1]

Activity Models

Activity diagrams, which were initially discussed in Chapter 2, display the actual flows represented in the use case. They go into deeper detail on how the flow of the system will work. They use swimlanes (the vertical and sometimes horizontal lines) to help you understand who or what is responsible for performing the activity. When you understand the responsibilities, you can then use that information to determine classes you will need to capture as logical data elements. The things defined by swimlanes often require data to be captured when the system is put into place.

The activity diagram shown in Figure 6-5 provides more insight to the conceptual data. We now see that the External Care Provider can review (read), update, and return (send) the Clinical Records. The Facility Staff can provide (send) and receive the Clinical Records.

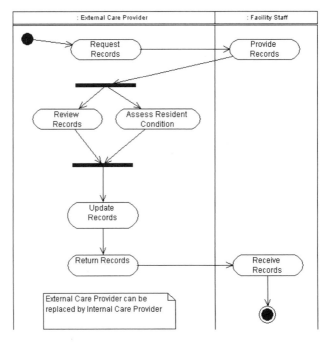

Figure 6-5 *Activity diagram for the Provide Clinical Care use case.*

In Figure 6-6, the activity diagram demonstrates how we can find new conceptual data—Billing Records and Reimbursement Records. Also, note that eligibility might be a possible attribute of a treatment (another candidate data entity). As before, we also see which business actors can manipulate this data, providing additional insight on how to design the database for the best performance and usage. [NAIB2]

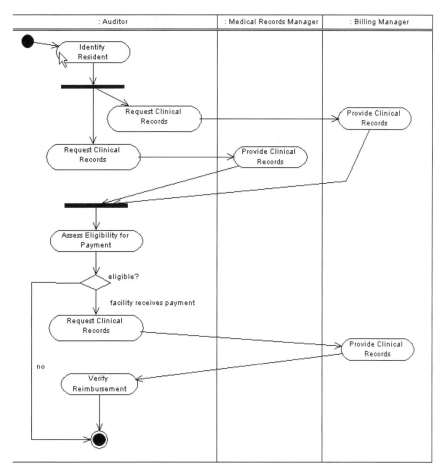

Figure 6-6 *Activity diagram for the Accounts Receivable use case for reimbursement.*

The activity diagram is often thought of as just showing the workflow, but as you can see in Figure 6-6, you can also use it to gain a greater understanding of how the system will be used and of the different entities that will be needed as the system evolves. Using structures such as swimlanes, the activity diagram provides the first set of elements needed to describe a complete logical database diagram. Yes, you can build a database design, either logical or physical, without use case and activity diagrams, but having them will help. Many of your organizations are already creating these diagrams, and the diagrams can help you build better database designs, so why not take advantage of them? Use these models to enhance your understanding of the overall system being created and what other team members have already discovered.

Class Models

Class diagrams and the elements used within them were introduced in Chapter 4 when we began talking about architecture. The database designers can leverage class models created by architects and developers to understand what the architecture of the application will look like and how they might translate the models into the logical data models. A database designer can also use the class models to create his own conceptual, logical, and physical data models. We will look closer at the data models later in this chapter. In this section, we will briefly cover how to take advantage of those models already created by others.

Class models are created by architects to design application architectures and by developers to visualize the pieces of the applications they are developing and the parts others have created so that they understand how to integrate with them. As described in Chapter 4, the architect will capture the designs of the application at a higher level, but these designs play very nicely into the creation of the conceptual and logical data models. Having the higher-level models provides the database team with guidance concerning entities and information about the data that they are going to need to capture.

Class diagrams created by developers show the planned and actual structure of the application. These diagrams show the business logic that will be implemented through the application class structures and the ways the application should interface with other software and the database. Database designers can take advantage of these diagrams to gain knowledge about how to implement business rules within the database and how to architect the database to best provide application access, and to ensure that the database provides the data storage for all the information to be supplied by the application.

All in all, being able to leverage information that's used by other teams will provide a database designer with additional input to building the database. A lot of work goes into building an overall system, and anything that can be shared will provide open communication among the team to help ensure that they are all working in a consistent direction. It isn't necessary that all the database designers be working in the UML, but having the team understand the UML will enable them to communicate with other teams about work that they have already done.

What Types of Database Models Can Be Created Using the UML?

Traditionally, there are three types of database design models:

1. Conceptual
2. Logical
3. Physical

All these can be modeled and designed using the UML. Not only can you create the traditional database models using the UML, but you can also create additional ones that once might have only been created on white boards or in the minds of the people responsible for the database. These models include how the database will be deployed, how applications will interact with the database, and even what hardware will be used and how the database server software will be deployed on that hardware.

As we continue with this chapter, we will focus on how to use the UML to create database designs and what elements can be used for them. Because this is just one chapter and not really a complete treatment of the subject, some details will be left out. For full details, see our book *UML for Database Design*.

Conceptual Models

A conceptual model is a very high-level model of a database. It typically models high-level domain entities and their basic relationships with other major domain entities. Its main purpose is to define the scope of the database while gaining an understanding of the data that needs to be captured. This model should be technology-independent.

Business Analysis Model

The conceptual model is first determined in the business analysis model. If your team is using UML for analysis and design, they most likely already have created business analysis models that can be leveraged and altered to define the conceptual data model. Even if business analysis models haven't already been created by others earlier in the process, they can be built now to define the conceptual data model.

A business entity is shown on a diagram as a circle with a line underneath and a line slashed through it (see Figure 6-7). The line at the bottom means it is an entity, and the slash shows that it is a business model. An advantage of using UML over traditional data modeling notations is that you can have different models that represent the different levels (i.e., business, analysis, implementation) of the model, rather than just different views of the same model.

Figure 6-7   *Business entity.*

The business entity itself in UML is a *class* with the stereotype of *<<business entity>>*. The icon that we described in the previous paragraph is associated with a business entity and is tied directly to that stereotype. If you are using a UML tool, it will in most cases have the business entity stereotype available for your use. If not, you can just create it and use it from then on. This is another value of the UML. Visually, the business entity looks different, whether it is by showing the textual version of the class with its stereotype or by seeing the icon that is associated with a particular stereotype, as shown in Figure 6-8.

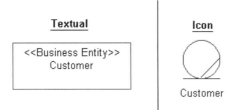

Figure 6-8   *Business entity stereotype.*

The business model is used as the conceptual model because the business entities represent the business view of the data model. Not to be confused with a business process model, which demonstrates how the business works using workflows and business rules, the business analysis model provides a view of the data that needs to be captured at the highest level.

Defining a Conceptual Model

To define a conceptual model, begin by figuring out the data that you want to capture. You must look at it from the highest level without trying to clarify any of the entities' properties but their names, often expressed in a natural language. While defining the entities, you will also begin to design relationships between these entities using the UML *associations*. Figure 6-9 provides an example of a conceptual data model that describes a part of a customer order system.

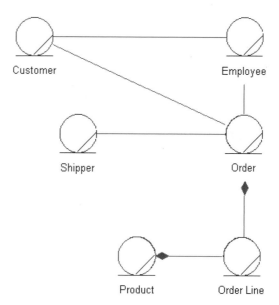

Figure 6-9   *Conceptual model.*

By using the UML to define the conceptual model, both the UML and the conceptual models created can be used by more than just one subgroup involved in development. The data modelers certainly use it as their conceptual data model, but the other teams can take advantage of it as well. For the analysts, it defines the business objects in the organization whose problem they are trying to solve with the software that is being built. It also helps to work with customers (either internal or external) to show them what you are building and to ensure that you capture all the information they deem necessary. Because it is at the conceptual level, they don't get caught up or even lost in the technical details. They get a high-level understanding of what is being designed. The software architects can also take advantage of this conceptual model to jump-start the application architecture they need to define. As the application needs to create, read, update, and delete (CRUD) information within the database, it is natural that the application and the database are conceptualized using the same information and process flow. As we described in the earlier real-world example "Taking Off with a Common Understanding," ensuring that the overall development team is starting with a common definition will go a long way toward success.

Watch Out—Trying to Please Everyone

Although we emphasize the value of keeping the entire team involved in creating the conceptual model, you also need to ensure that you're not trying to create something that is all things to all parties involved. The conceptual data model has a purpose, and you don't want to drift from that purpose by trying to follow a process that satisfies everyone. The intention from the beginning should be to qualify the requirements. True, the elements that are being defined as database entities should also be the same entities, at least conceptually, that you need to capture for the application. That being said, though, you don't want to create a model that ends up having no meaning because you were trying to have meanings for everyone.

The point is to make sure that you scope the work. It is great to work together in defining a common conceptual model as the airline did, but they were also smart about it and defined a vision for what is expected from the conceptual model as well as rules regarding its intent. When you know your boundaries, it is much easier to ensure that your conceptual model doesn't become just a dumping ground for all business-level entities that might have nothing to do with the project or database.

Logical Models

Logical modeling is used to design the application or, in this case, the database, at a technology-independent level. The logical data model generally uses non-technical names for *entities,* much like the *business entities* in the conceptual model, and does not at this point concern itself with how the database will be implemented. The logical model is used to communicate the designs at a level that the implementers of the database can use to transform that model into a high-performing database specific to the platform they use, no matter what target database management system (DBMS) is used.

Database design tools often provide capabilities to transform the conceptual model into the logical model, maintaining mappings of the entities as they evolve through time to ensure that the requirement's intent wasn't changed in implementation. Using UML or any modeling language that contains a common meta-model for objects, you can provide linkage or traceability from one entity to another, even though it might morph into something else over time.

Deep Dive—Moving from Conceptual to Logical

Morphing conceptual model entities into logical ones might be as straightforward as using basically the same entity with the same name and properties, or it could become a number of different entities all mapped back to that same business entity in the conceptual model. For example, you might have a business entity called "customer," and that is fine for the conceptual model. But when you start to define the logical model for database consistency, you might determine that you need to capture data for several different types of customers with different data. Because of this, you might decide that you will have three different logical entities: retail customer, wholesale customer, and online customer. The three are mapped back to that one conceptual model element called customer, but there is also great value in knowing that mapping. When reviewing the conceptual and logical models, you can ensure consistency where needed and work with your client (as well as the other teams involved) to be sure they are in agreement with the different types of customers.

A logical model will also start to fill in some of the pieces that were not important to the conceptual model. One of the major additions to the logical model when compared to the conceptual one is *attributes*. Attributes define the properties of an entity in greater detail. Keeping with the customer exam-ple, attributes of a customer could include name, address, phone number, and more. Attributes also have a *type* associated with them for further descrip-tion. A type describes an attribute—for example, the attribute name is described as a "text" type, meaning that data captured for a name must be in text format. Databases support specific datatypes, which we will talk about in the "Physical Modelings" section of this chapter. For now, in the logical model, we will stay with more generic types.

Class Diagrams

You might have already figured it out, but just in case you haven't, class dia-grams are used for logical models and logical database designs. The class dia-gram encompasses all the constructs needed to build a logical database design. Classes for attributes with the stereotype of <<entity>>, along with attributes within that class, make up the logical database design construct of entity. The stereotype of entity can be viewed either in text form or using an icon, as you can see in Figure 6-10.

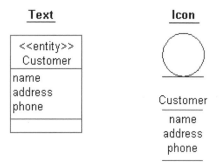

Figure 6-10   *Entity stereotypes.*

Although the icon tells you more quickly that the class is an entity, we don't recommend you use the icon, especially within a tool, unless you are showing the entity without attributes. As you saw in Figure 6-10, the addition of attrib-utes to the entity on a diagram with multiple entities can make it difficult to read. Using the textual version of the stereotype in these scenarios provides the definition of an entity without cluttering up the diagram. Quite often, you will have multiple diagrams that show the same entities in different ways. You might have a diagram that is set up just to review entities and their names and relations. In that case, simply displaying the name is sufficient, while other diagrams that use that exact same entity could require further detail.

Three basic types of relationships are used in a logical data model. Traditionally, when designing a database, you will have the following types of relationships:

- **Non-identifying**—A relationship in which the child and parent entities can exist on their own without each other.
- **Identifying**—A relationship in which the child entity cannot exist without its parent.
- **Inheritance**—A relationship in which the child entity, or quite often multiple child entities, inherit by its relationship everything that is included in the parent entity.

Table 6-1 shows how these traditional database design relationships are represented in the UML.

Table 6-1 *Mapping of Traditional Database Design Relationships to Those in UML*

Traditional Database Design	UML
Non-identifying	Association
Identifying	Composite aggregation
Inheritance	Generalization

The non-identifying and identifying relationships use both the UML relationship type noted in Table 6-1 and a stereotype that denotes the type of relationship. Because each relationship type is graphically distinct, you can use your judgment as to whether the display of the stereotype is needed on the diagram. Figure 6-11 provides UML notation for each of the relationships described.

Figure 6-11 *Logical relationships.*

When defining the logical data model, you will also define business rules that can be enforced in the database. One such business rule is known as cardinality (a.k.a. multiplicity). As explained earlier in this chapter, multiplicity more deeply defines the relationship between two entities to essentially show the number of instances involved in a given relationship. For example, one customer can place one or more orders, but an order can only be placed by one customer.

Watch Out—Counting the Customers

The UML uses the word "multiplicity," whereas database designers traditionally call the same thing "cardinality." Don't get caught up in the words; just make sure you capture the multiplicity or cardinality correctly. Whether you follow the UML by the book or you stay with what you and the rest of your team are familiar with does not matter. However, keep it consistent across the team so everybody is on the same page.

Chapter 3, "Requirements Modeling," goes into more depth describing the different types of multiplicity and how they are used, so refer back to that chapter for additional details.

As the class is used to define an entity, you will use several classes to describe the overall logical data model. Because the UML provides the ability to create multiple diagrams within a single model, you can use each of these diagrams to demonstrate different uses for each entity. For example, you can have the same entity present on multiple diagrams, but you can use them to show different things. One diagram might be used to describe the customer relationship aspects of the database, while another might be used to describe marketing aspects. The customer entity can occur on both diagrams, and it still has the same meaning, but the diagrams describe different areas of the database. Figure 6-12 shows a portion of the marketing diagram. The customer relationship diagram contains the use of all the different logical modeling elements we have talked about so far in this chapter.

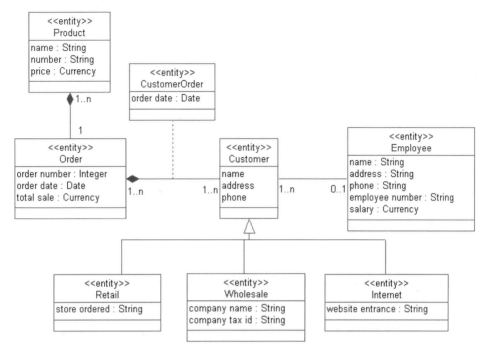

Figure 6-12 · *Customer relationship logical database diagram.*

Primary keys are used to uniquely define a logical entity. The primary key is an attribute that is unique for any particular row entered within a database. For example, you can have many orders, but generally, there is only one order number per order, and each order has a different number. A primary key in the UML contains a stereotype of <<primary key>>. This stereotype both provides properties specific to a primary key and also gives a visual cue to the fact that it is a primary key. To save room on a particular diagram, we have seen different tools use different variations on the stereotype. Some spell it out entirely, and others shorten it by just using the initials as <<PK>> for the stereotype. Figure 6-13 shows the customer relationship model again with primary keys added.

The logical model leads to the physical model, which we will cover in the next section. Although it goes against best practices, teams often create a logical model one time and never go back to it. They then move from the logical to the physical and only work in the physical model thereafter. The value of the logical model is to ensure that what you are building is the right thing for the business, and it serves as a communication vehicle for the different constituencies to share, including programmers, analysts, etc. By only working in the physical model after a first logical model is created, you run the risk of implementing a database specifically for physical reasons, and you miss out on opportunities to ensure the business needs are synchronized with what is being implemented.

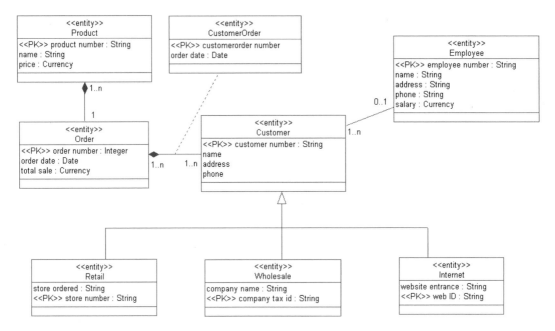

Figure 6-13 *Primary keys in the logical model.*

Physical Modelings

Physical database design is tied directly to the implementation of the database. The data model that is created for the physical database takes into account the specifics of the DBMS and is optimized for such software and hardware.

Logical Versus Physical

Where the logical model has entities, the physical model has tables, which are the physical implementation of entities. Just like entities and tables, attributes, which are logical, become columns in the physical model.

Most databases don't support inheritance as it is described in the logical model. Therefore, decisions need to be made when moving to the implementation. To rid yourself of inheritance in the physical model, you have a few common choices:

- **One-to-one** mapping of each entity in the inheritance to a table. Here, you will create additional columns in the tables and have identifying relationships between the child tables and the parent super-type table.
- **Roll-up**, in which all the subtypes (child tables) are rolled up into the parent table, making just one table. The single table will have columns that differentiate themselves to show the different subtypes. For example, instead of having both fulltime and part-time employees, the employee table might have a column called employee type.
- **Roll-down**, in which the parent table no longer exists in the transformation, but all or most of the columns in the parent table are created in *each* of the child tables. Regarding the previous example, in this case, there would be a fulltime and part-time table, but there would no longer be an employee table. The columns that would have been just in the employee table, like name, address, and so forth, would now be included in both the fulltime and part-time tables.

Data types are another difference between the logical and physical database models. Where in the logical you have generic types, in the physical, types are specific to the database vendor. Most vendors support a standard set of types, but to add competitive differentiation, each vendor provides additional types that add value to their platforms.

The last difference that we will cover is foreign keys. Foreign keys describe the relationships between tables. They are the migration of the primary key from the parent table into the foreign key of the child table. The foreign key can become part of either the primary key in the child table or just a regular column, depending on the relationship between the two tables. An identifying relationship means that the foreign key will also be a primary key, while a non-identifying relationship means it is just a foreign key. There are many other differences between the two types of models, but these are the primary ones that we will cover in this book.

Physical Data Models

Just like in the logical model, physical data models are described using classes and class diagrams. Stereotypes in the physical model include <<table>> to show that the class is a table and either <<foreign key>> or <<FK>> to denote a foreign key.

One of the values of using the UML to define database designs is the additional constructs that are available as compared to other database modeling notations. Having the extra compartment where operations are modeled in a class provides the ability to capture information in the physical model that cannot be visualized in traditional data modeling notations. *Indexes* and *constraints* are physical implementations that traditionally are not modeled anywhere but are just hidden in the meta-data of a physical model. The UML provides the ability to model indexes and constraints and enables the team to visualize these elements so that you are doing more with the models and allowing everyone who needs to understand how the database is being implemented to do so visually. Referential integrity constraints that provide information on primary and foreign keys are used, as are indexes and check constraints. The stereotypes used for these constraints are <<PK>>, <<FK>>, <<Index>>, and <<Check>>. Also, triggers are defined as operations on a table using the stereotype of <<Trigger>>. These are the main stereotypes used in the physical model that differ from the logical. Figure 6-14 shows the different stereotypes and icons used in the physical data model.

Just like the transformations used for inheritance, you will choose how to transform other entities into tables. You might want to have one-to-one mappings, but you might decide for performance improvement, security, or other reasons to alter your transformations to other than a one-to-one mapping. The concepts of splitting a single entity into more than one is common for reasons of searching and performance as well as doing the opposite, that is, combining multiple tables into one.

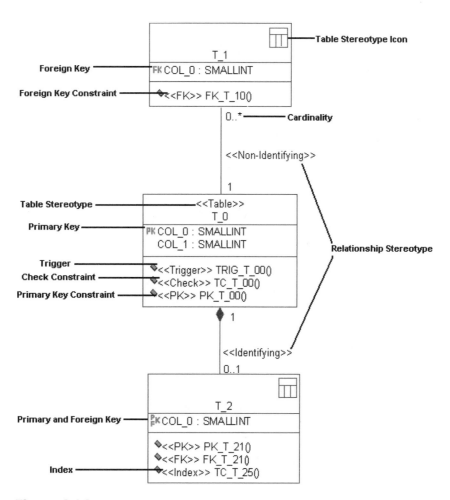

Figure 6-14 *Physical data model.*

Topics to Consider

You might want to consider these additional topics:

- **Sequence diagrams**—Consider how sequence diagrams can help you to determine index creation and flow of data.
- **Deployment diagrams**—Understand how databases are deployed to different hardware and are used across the systems.
- **Database design techniques**—Learn these ways of creating good database designs outside of modeling notations and languages.

Terms

Business object	Cardinality
Conceptual	Multiplicity
Physical	Generalization
Database	Composite aggregation
Check constraint	Roll-up
Foreign key	Roll-down
Class	Key constraint
Attribute	Logical
Table	Index
Column	Trigger
Identifying	Constraint
Non-identifying	Primary key

Summary

This chapter started with a discussion of the different ways to model databases and how they all show pretty much the same things, no matter what your notation. We demonstrated the similarities between IE, IDEF1X, and UML and how each depicts the same models in a different way.

From the understanding of different modeling types, we entered into the view that no matter what your role, you should involve everyone in software development, whether they are analysts, developers, architects, or database designers, and that each member must have a common understanding and work together to define each element. By working together, you ensure that different groups are not, for example, using the same name to describe a different thing (or vice versa) and also that they can reuse each other's work. Whether you decide to use UML for your database designs or not, leveraging the work of others has tremendous value. Having the database designers understand UML and the work that the analysts and architects have defined will enable the database team to jump-start their designs and ensure that the requirements uncovered for the project are common across the teams.

We then looked at how to create conceptual, logical, and physical data models using the UML. We started with business analysis models to create the conceptual and moved into class diagrams for the logical and physical. Several stereotypes are available in the UML for database design. These stereotypes are used to both visually describe and provide additional properties to these stereotyped elements, enabling database design.

Overall, whether you select to model the database using UML or just decide to leverage what already exists from other teams, understanding UML has great value. Keeping teams synchronized and driving toward common goals is what database applications need to succeed.

Review Questions

1. Which one isn't a way to model databases?
   a. UML
   b. IDEF1X
   c. PBC
   d. IE

2. What type of model describes the conceptual data model?

3. True or False: A class is stereotyped as <<entity>> in the logical data model.

4. True or False: A class is stereotyped as <<trigger>> in the physical data model.

5. Name three types of stereotypes used on a class during database design.

[NAIB1] [NAIB2] Naiburg, Eric J. and Robert A. Maksimchuk. 2001. *UML for Database Design*. Boston, MA: Addison-Wesley.

7

Testing

Topics Covered in This Chapter

How Can the UML Help Me in Testing?

How Can I Use the Business Use Case Models?

    System, Integration, and Subsystem Testing

How Can I Use the Business Analysis Models?

    Integration and Subsystem Testing

How Can I Use the Analysis and Design Models?

    Unit, Class, and Algorithmic Testing

What About Other Types of Testing?

    Performance and Regression Testing

Topics to Consider

Terms

Summary

Review Questions

How Can the UML Help Me in Testing?

Many people do not associate the UML with testing activities on a project. This is not surprising. For decades, the commitment to rigorous testing has received spotty support, usually in favor of meeting the schedule commitments on projects. This mindset arises from decades of de-emphasizing the importance of testing. Although there have been various industry-wide quality initiatives such as Total Quality Management, Six Sigma, and so forth, testing often takes a back seat to the other activities in systems development. One of the main factors causing this is timing—people focus on what they perceive is urgent. As Alexander Kossiakoff and William N. Sweet say in *Systems Engineering Principles and Practice,* "Test planning is seldom allocated adequate priority in either staffing or funding in the early phases of system development." [KOSS1] Testing is often thought of as an activity that happens later in the development lifecycle, after coding. Early in the development lifecycle, teams focus on the more immediate issues, such as architecture, design, and so forth. By the time the team gets to the "testing phase" of the project, schedule slips have already occurred, so this time is made up by shrinking the time allotted for testing. This typical scenario illustrates how the importance of testing is compromised for other "urgent" project issues.

We contend that testing should not be relegated to the tail end of a project. We believe people involved in the testing effort should be involved *at the beginning* of the project through to the delivery of the final product. Involving the test personnel at the beginning, as early as the business modeling stage, will help prevent errors from being introduced into your system in the first place. As Stephen Covey said about focusing on what is important (in our case, testing) over what is urgent:

> Your effectiveness would increase dramatically. Your crises and problems would shrink to manageable proportions because you would be thinking ahead, working on the roots, doing the preventive things that keep situations from developing into crises in the first place. [COVE1]

From the Real World—Hey Joe! Where You Goin' with That Plan in Your Hand?

During my software development career, I have managed and otherwise worked alongside many test (a.k.a. "quality assurance") people. Of all these folks, one gentleman stood out as the absolute best testing person I have ever met. I was a software engineer on a large, real-time system development project when I met Joe. Joe was assigned to be our test guy. He had a couple of decades on all of us young hot shots. He was not an expert on our particular domain area, but he had worked in other areas of the program.

Joe was quite different from other test people our team had encountered. Besides the age difference, Joe was a real high-energy guy—always curious, always asking questions. Joe injected himself in discussions regarding what we were doing even before we had our requirements established. Throughout the development, Joe was there looking for ways to help us, asking about changes we were making, how the software should operate, and otherwise steeping himself in our part of the development.

As we approached code completion, Joe was ready. He always asked us if we had an early code build that he could "play with." He would sit for hours learning how our subsystem operated. With his earlier knowledge of how the software was required to operate and his hands-on involvement, he provided a number of valuable services to our group during the "traditional" testing phase. His input improved the quality of our test plans and procedures. As he "played" with the software, he "scrubbed" the test data, improving its quality, and he questioned why things operated as they did, which led us, in some cases, to actually change the designs. He did all this prior to actually executing formal tests.

When he did run the tests, we could be sure that if he wrote a defect against our software, it was a valid one. When he would find a problem, he would investigate it with a few more trials instead of just immediately submitting a defect. His preemptive investigation of problems saved us a great deal of time on our subsequent technical investigation of the defects. His depth of knowledge, gained by being involved at the beginning of the project, not only enabled all this but also made him very efficient. He could get multiple test runs completed in the time that an average tester could run a test once. We taught him. He taught us. And our defect counts during system testing were typically the lowest on the project.

Lessons Learned

1. Get your test folks involved as early as possible in your development. (And when using UML, ensure they are involved early so they can understand your models, be immediately productive, and leverage the models you build.)

So, how exactly can you as a test professional (or software developer) use the UML to help your test activities? The good news is that the UML models developed by the analysts, architects, and designers in the early phases of a project can be directly used to jump-start testing activities.

How Can I Use the Business Use Case Models?

As we discussed in Chapter 2, business use case models provide the context in which your business operates. They serve as a context diagram for your business, depicting what is outside of your business (the business actors), what is inside the business (the business use cases), and their relationships (see Figure 7-1).

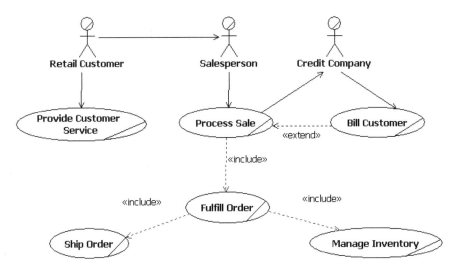

Figure 7-1   *Business use case diagram.*

Business use cases are a source of *candidate subsystems* in the *architecture* of your system. The business use case diagram in Figure 7-1 might yield part of the system architecture as shown in Figure 7-2. Note that there is not necessarily a one-for-one relationship here. Every business use case does not necessarily become a subsystem. Multiple subsystems could be created for each business use case, or one subsystem could be derived from more than one business use case. This is why we say they are "candidate" subsystems—they are just a starting point for an architecture that will evolve during its development.

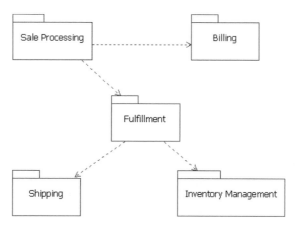

Figure 7-2 *System architecture diagram.*

System, Integration, and Subsystem Testing

This system architecture and its candidate subsystems can help you structure your testing. Where you focus establishes the structure and scope of your testing. For example, if you focus on the individual subsystems and their particular actors, you're performing a *subsystem test*. If you look at subsystems in combination, these provide the basis for *integration tests* between these subsystems. When you test all subsystems together, you're performing a *system level test* (see Figure 7-3).

The business actors in these models are the roles that testers can assume for testing purposes. What should these testers do? They can establish the specific test procedures using the activity diagrams that were developed as part of the business use case model. Remembering that the activity diagram scenarios in the business use case model depict the interaction between your *external* users and the system, they provide the basis for *black box testing*. Black box testing focuses on testing the externally visible behavior of the system (or element of the system) without knowledge of the internal structure of the element.

As we noted earlier, the business use case model can provide organization and structure to your test planning. You can easily identify candidate test plans based on the subsystems or combinations thereof. The activity diagrams of the business use case model can also provide a great start to the development of test procedures. The flows defined in the diagrams can provide the core of your test procedures, offering a great jump-start to their development.

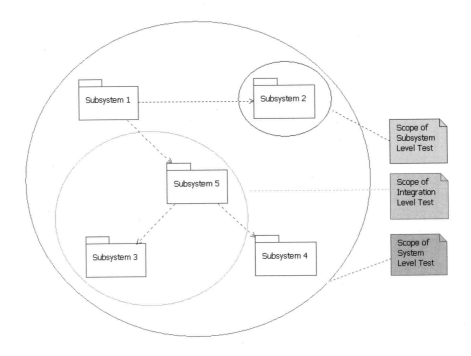

Figure 7-3   *Test scope.*

Of course, you will need to add further details based on the standard information you include in your procedures. The activity diagrams can help to identify some of that additional information. For example, let's revisit the activity diagram from Chapter 2 for processing a sale (see Figure 7-4).

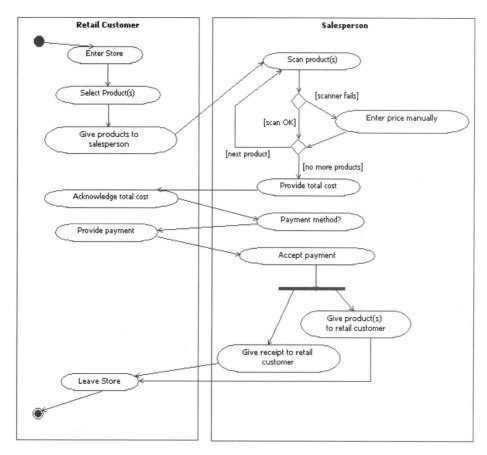

Figure 7-4   *Retail sale activity diagram.*

Activity diagrams can indicate places to define ranges of test data to use in your test scenarios. A good place to start is where the flows cross over between swimlanes (highlighted in Figure 7-5). Data and control information are often related to the activities that are connected by these flows.

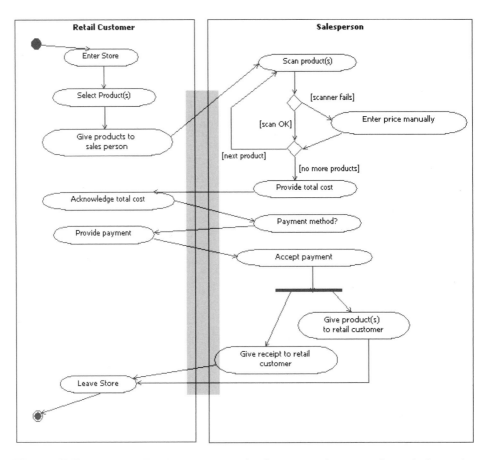

Figure 7-5   *Looking for data or control information between the swimlanes in activity diagrams.*

For example, one activity asks for the "Payment Method." This obviously leads you to a range of values for payment method, such as cash, credit, check, and maybe some less obvious ones, such as gift certificate or gift card, cashier's check, store credit voucher, and so forth. What about the activity "Give receipt to retail customer?" If that receipt is not given (i.e., nothing flows across the swimlanes), what happens? Consider the activity "Provide total cost." Where does it get the cost to provide to the customer? This leads back to the activity "Enter price manually." What actual prices would you use in testing? Don't forget boundary testing, that is, using test data that is at the extremes of the expected data range, particularly just beyond, at, and just within the upper and lower bounds of the data range. In this case, what happens if you enter

$0.00 as a price? Can you enter a price such as "three for $1.00?" This question leads you to think about your expected results. If you buy two items at "three for $1.00," at what level of precision do you expect the "Provide total cost" activity to provide the cost to the customer? When dealing with prices, you might expect an answer to two decimal places. But you need to verify that. And what about numeric rounding?

As with most visual models, activity diagrams can trigger a tremendously beneficial amount of critical thinking. In fact, as you use these diagrams to help create your test procedures, you are likely to find additional alternate paths that the designers might have overlooked. UML diagrams can provide a point of focus that no text-only representation can provide.

How Can I Use the Business Analysis Models?

While the business use case model provides the external view of your business, the business analysis model provides the view of what your business does internally. As you might recall, the business analysis model elements are those people and things inside your business that perform the activities to satisfy the requests made upon your business. (See Figure 7-6, which depicts a business analysis model we showed you in Chapter 2.)

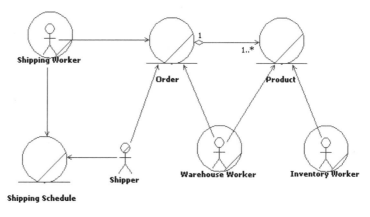

Figure 7-6 *Business analysis model (partial) for retail system.*

In this case, this business analysis model shows what happens *inside* your business to fulfill an order. This obviously leads us to realize that the business analysis model can help establish the white box tests of your system. *White box testing* focuses on testing the internals of the system (i.e. elements that exist inside your subsystems). One possible architecture is shown in Figure 7-7.

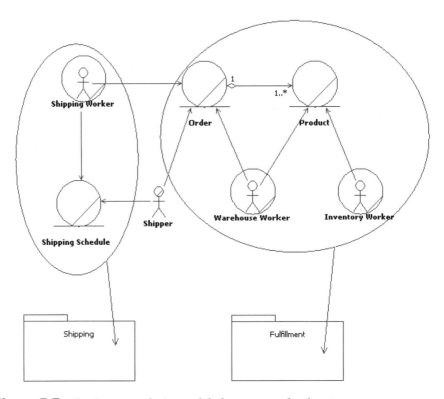

Figure 7-7   *Business analysis model elements and subsystems.*

Integration and Subsystem Testing

As with black box testing, your focus during white box testing determines the scope and structure of the white box testing you will perform. If you focus on the individual subsystems and their particular business workers, then you have a subsystem white box test. If you look at subsystems in combination, these provide the basis for white box integration tests between these subsystems (if there is a need to do such detailed testing at an integration level). When you take all subsystems together, you have a system-level white box test. Keep in mind that in a system of significant size, such a system-level white box test might be prohibitively complex. However, such an approach would provide a great way to validate your architecture early in the development. Some wise advice: "Test the architecture by using the scenarios to walk through the system. Does this work? Do you have all the interfaces you need to implement the scenarios?" [SCHN1]

Details for these white box test procedures can come from the business analysis model's sequence diagrams. They indicate the flow of control and messages between the elements in your model, providing a jump-start to test procedure development. As with the activity diagrams for white box testing, you might need to add additional testing details to your procedures. You can augment the sequence diagrams to add that additional information. For example, let's revisit the sequence diagram from Chapter 2 for creating an order (see Figure 7-8).

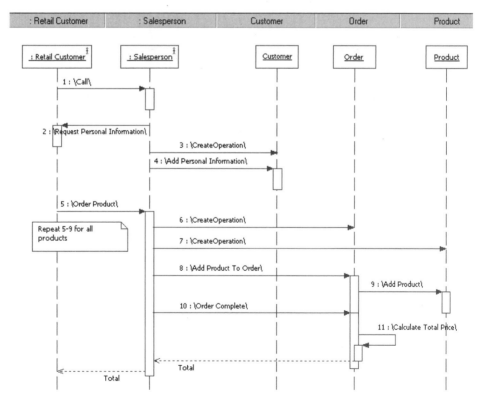

Figure 7-8   *Sequence diagram for creating an order for a retail sale.*

The sequence diagram flow provides the basic test flow for this scenario. Each message flowing between the model elements is a potential place for further elaboration. If the message is providing data at a given point (such as "Add Personal Information" in Figure 7-8), you could test various data ranges there. If the message indicates the system is performing certain processing (such as "Calculate Total Price" in Figure 7-8), you must consider whether you should test performance requirements there. If the system must return the Total Price within 10 seconds, you can annotate this diagram appropriately. Control flows (such as "Add Product to Order" in Figure 7-8) provide excellent opportunities to examine possible alternate flows. Hopefully, whoever created these diagrams already considered such alternate flows. But if not, here is another opportunity for test people to affect the system design early in the development lifecycle, helping create a more robust and higher quality system (see the test-related annotations in Figure 7-9).

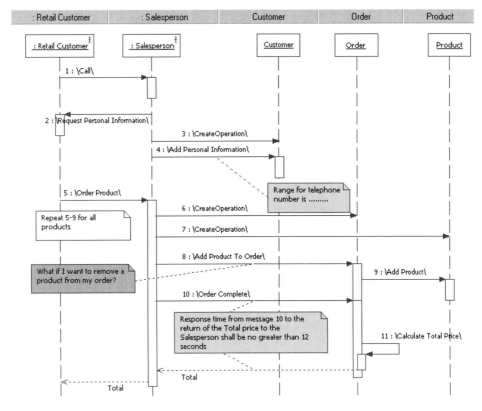

Figure 7-9   *Annotated sequence diagram for a retail sale (creating an order).*

Deep Dive—Database Testing—Move On Up

As mentioned earlier, sequence diagrams are probably the most versatile and useful diagrams in the UML. Not only do they serve their intended function of showing a time-ordered sequence of collaboration between the elements of the system, and not only can they help provide details for test procedures, but they can also help to test the database. How? A *database transaction* is "an action or series of actions, carried out by a single user or application program, which accesses or changes the contents of the database." [CONN1] Look back at Figure 7-8. In it, a user (Salesperson) creates, changes, and accesses various business entities (i.e., Order, Product, Customer). Sequence diagrams can be diagrams of your database transactions.

Realize that these are high-level (business-level) diagrams. Order, Product, and Customer are *domain entities* that are key to your business operation. In the actual implementation of the database, more tables likely will be involved in such a transaction. During database implementation, the database design typically is significantly modified from its logical or conceptual design. However, these sequence diagrams depict what needs to be done from a *business* point of view. You can use them to determine if these business transaction scenarios can actually work after the detailed database implementation is complete. You should consider whether your implemented database can support these intended business functions. Sequence diagrams provide a basis for your database validation. Just as test people should be involved early in the lifecycle, database analysts should also be moved up to the early stages of development to help in the definition of such sequences.

How Can I Use the Analysis and Design Models?

The use of UML analysis and design models as part of testing is straightforward. You use these diagrams to design the low-level components of your system. Therefore, these diagrams can directly aid in *unit testing*—that is, the testing of the individual system components prior to integration with others, typically performed by the developer who has created the component.

Consider the use case diagram in Figure 7-10. This is a use case diagram of a subsystem, which is part of a medical records system that is responsible for compliance with state regulations. [NAIB3] (Note: An MDS [Minimum Data Set] is a specific extraction of certain information from the clinical records of a patient.)

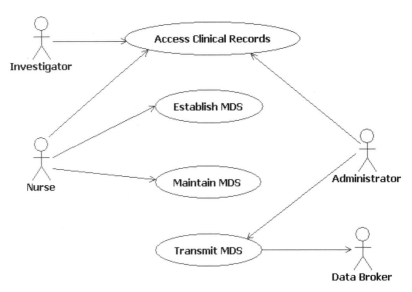

Figure 7-10 *Use case diagram of compliance subsystem.*

Unit, Class, and Algorithmic Testing

Use cases are a representation of your requirements. Thus, each of these use cases can provide the details for individual unit test plans As you develop these use cases, you create use case specifications (textual), sequence diagrams, class diagrams, and possibly other UML diagrams. The use case specifications and sequence diagrams (see Figure 7-11) can fill in the details of the unit test procedure for these use cases, similar to what we discussed earlier in this chapter for higher-level testing.

These design diagrams, used in conjunction with the related class diagrams (see Figure 7-12), can form the basis for the detailed structural (i.e., white box) testing of this specific component and its classes.

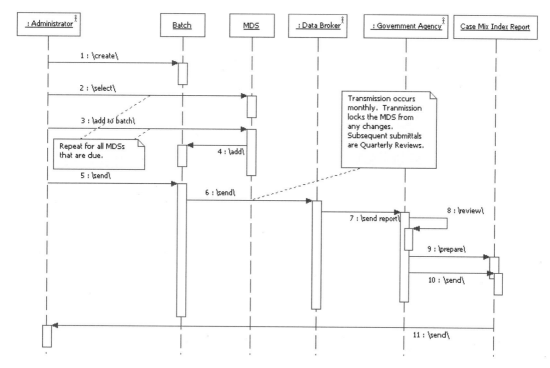

Figure 7-11   *Transmit MDS sequence diagram. [NAIB4]*

If you are testing classes individually, additional UML diagrams can help. For example, an activity diagram can help design and document a complex mathematical algorithm performed by a class. Such a diagram would map out the flow and steps of the algorithm. If a class has particularly complex behavior or is event-driven, you can depict the manner in which this class operates with a statechart diagram, which depicts the state of an object, the actions it performs, and the events that trigger it to change its state. Figure 7-13 shows a statechart for a transaction, specifically the processing of an order to buy a security.

You can use the statechart to direct how to drive the testing of the class (actually, an object) by creating the various events shown on the transitions (i.e., the arrows). This enables you to verify that the class is processing correctly. Indeed, some modern modeling tools you to automate the creation of statechart diagrams for testing purposes.) You will learn more about statecharts (called state machine diagrams in UML 2.0) in Chapter 8, "Is That All There Is?."

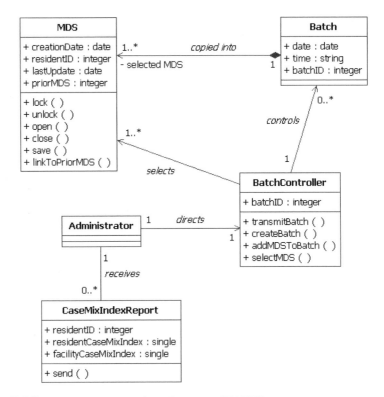

Figure 7-12   *Transmit MDS class diagram. [NAIB5]*

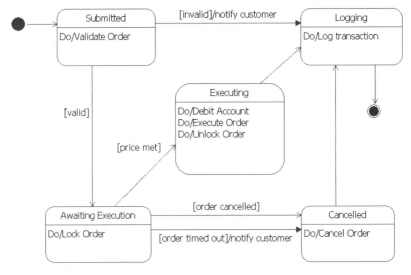

Figure 7-13   *Statechart for a securities transaction.*

What About Other Types of Testing?

Some UML diagrams can also help you with *non-functional testing*. We previously discussed the annotation of activity and sequence diagrams when performance requirements need to be tested (e.g., response time, processing time, delays). As you levy *performance* requirements on a system, you can make explicit the "budgeting" (i.e., allocation) of those requirements to the various lower-level components directly on the appropriate UML diagram. (Also, in UML 2.0, numerous additions have been made related to time—the new timing diagrams, enhancements to sequence diagrams and state machine diagrams, and so forth.)

Performance and Regression Testing

UML can also help you understand performance issues early in development, before it is too late. Examine your sequence diagrams. If you notice in your model (not just in one diagram) that a particular element has many, many messages flowing to it, this might indicate that this element might have a performance problem. For example, if the element is a system log that many elements in the system are writing to and reading from it at the same time, this could be a problem. Design changes should be considered in such cases. Notwithstanding, if we are doing testing and the sequence diagrams show such a situation, they are clearly pointing out that this element should be load tested.

Your UML models can also guide *regression testing*. A regression test is a test (or set of tests) that you run after someone makes a change to your system in order to ensure that the system still operates correctly. When someone changes something in your system, you can use the models to determine which regression tests you need to perform or even which new tests you need to run to test the changes. For example, referring back to Figure 7-12, if someone makes a change to the BatchController, you don't just test that controller in isolation. You should execute a regression test to ensure that it still collaborates correctly with all the other elements it is involved with, which you can identify in the UML class diagram. To be thorough, the entire Transmit MDS use case should be the regression test. However, in some cases, the related use case can be very complex. If you need to limit the scope of the regression testing, you could find the sequences (and alternate flows) in the use case's sequence diagrams that involve BatchController and retest only those flows.

Topics to Consider

You might want to examine these additional topics:

- As discussed in Chapter 5, "Application Modeling," classes can exist in a class hierarchy where the child classes inherit attributes and operations from their parent class. Child classes can override or change the operations they inherit. Also, many levels to such class hierarchies can exist. If a child class somewhere in the middle of a class hierarchy overrides an operation and subsequently that operation changes, how would this affect testing?
- Consider how UML could aid in user interface testing.
- If your system architecture changes, how can UML diagrams be used to determine the level of regression testing needed?
- If your system's overall architecture remains the same, but some system elements are moved from one subsystem to a different subsystem, how can UML diagrams be used to determine the level of regression testing needed?
- Examine the use of UML 2.0 timing diagrams.

Terms

Total Quality Management	Six Sigma
Urgent	Important
Business use case model	Business actor
Business analysis model	Business use case
Use case diagram	Architecture
System test	Integration test
Subsystem test	Unit test
Black box testing	White box testing
Activity diagram	Sequence diagram
Statechart diagram	Database testing

Transaction	Domain entity
Algorithm	Trigger
Transition	Non-functional testing
Performance testing	Regression testing
Hierarchy	Override

Summary

This chapter started with an explanation of the benefits associated with having test people involved very early in the system development lifecycle, much earlier than they are typically included. We discussed an example of how this involvement can improve the quality of the tests, reduce the effort in repairing defects, increase defect avoidance, and produce a higher quality system.

Then, we walked through the various UML models and diagrams with an eye to their use in testing. You learned how the business use case model and the system architecture that results from it can organize your system, integration, and subsystem black box test plans. Similarly, we saw how the business analysis model can establish your system, integration, and subsystem white box test plans.

We pointed out how the various UML diagrams in these models can provide the details of your test procedures and how these diagrams can be augmented with additional information important for testing.

You saw how the various analysis and design models provide the detail to guide the unit testing of individual system components. We ended with a discussion on the use of UML in performance and regression testing. This chapter demonstrated how you can use the UML diagrams that are created in the early development of the system to give yourself a head start in your testing program.

Review Questions

1. Whether the scope of a test comprises system, integration, or subsystem testing is primarily determined by:

   a. The number of use cases involved in the test

   b. The number of classes involved in the test

   c. The number of subsystems involved in the test

   d. The number of UML diagrams involved in the test

2. True or False: Detailed algorithmic processing can best be represented in a class diagram.

3. Testing that focuses on the internals of the component under test is known as:

   a. White box testing

   b. Regression testing

   c. Black box testing

   d. Non-functional testing

   e. Performance testing

4. The UML diagrams that can show how your test procedures should flow are:

   a. Statechart diagrams

   b. Activity diagrams

   c. Sequence diagrams

   d. a and b above

   e. b and c above

   f. a, b, and c above

   g. None of the above

5. True or False: Test personnel should become involved in the systems development after the detailed analysis and design models are complete.

6. Name a type of non-functional testing that can be aided by UML diagrams.

[CONN1] Connolly, Thomas M. and Carolyn E. Begg. 1999. *Database Systems: A Practical Approach to Design, Implementation, and Management.* Addison-Wesley.

[COVE1] Covey, Stephen R. 1989. *Seven Habits of Highly Effective People: Restoring the Character Ethic.* New York: Simon & Schuster.

[KOSS1] Kossiakoff, Alexander and William N. Sweet. 2003. *Systems Engineering Principles and Practice.* New Jersey: John Wiley & Sons, Inc.

[NAIB3] Adapted from a use case model by Naiburg, Eric J. and Robert A. Maksimchuk. 2001. *UML for Database Design.* Boston, MA: Addison-Wesley.

[NAIB4] Naiburg, Eric J. and Robert A. Maksimchuk. op. cit.

[NAIB5] Naiburg, Eric J. and Robert A. Maksimchuk. op. cit.

[SCHN1] Schneider, Geri and Jason P. Winters. 1998. *Applying Use Cases: A Practical Guide.* Addison-Wesley.

8

Is That All There Is?

Topics Covered in This Chapter

Other UML Diagrams

Statechart Diagrams

Collaboration Diagrams

Object Diagrams

More on UML 2.0

Changes to Collaboration Diagrams

Changes to Activity Diagrams

Changes to Sequence Diagrams

Changes to Component Diagrams

Changes to Class Diagrams

Topics to Consider

Terms

Summary

Review Questions

Introduction

In prior chapters, you learned how the UML can be applied to your specific job functions. In this chapter, you will learn about some less often used UML diagrams. We also will cover the new features in version 2.0 of the UML that mere mortals will most likely encounter and need to understand.

Other UML Diagrams

The UML contains several additional types of diagrams. And after the Object Management Group (www.omg.org/uml/) ratifies version 2.0 of the UML late in 2004, it will include several more (for the full list, see Chapter 1, "Introduction to the UML"). Although each diagram provides value, people use some of them more often than others. We focused the majority of this book on what software development teams have told us they most commonly use and the corresponding model elements so that you will be most familiar with those subjects and best able to communicate with your teams who are modeling with the UML.

In some cases, the diagrams covered so far in this book are appropriate for use by specific people and roles in an organization, such as developers, business analysts, and database designers, and in other cases, they are appropriate for the task at hand and are used by multiple groups in the organization. This section focuses on the "best of the rest"—which fall into both of the previous categories but primarily are used across different roles. These diagrams include statechart diagrams, collaboration diagrams, and object diagrams. We will explain what they consist of and how and when you would use them. These diagrams are valuable, but not as frequently used as the other diagrams discussed throughout the rest of this book.

Statechart Diagrams

A *state* is a condition during the life of an object or interaction during which it satisfies some condition, performs some action, or waits for some event. An *object* is an instance of a class. An object can move through many different states. An object can do any or all of the following in any specific state:

- Perform an activity (see Chapter 2, "Business Modeling," for details on activity modeling)
- Wait for an event
- Satisfy one or more conditions

Statechart diagrams (known as "state machine diagrams" in UML 2.0) model the dynamic behavior of individual objects or any other instance of a modeling element. They show the sequences of states that an object goes through, the events that cause a transition from one state to another, and the actions that can result from a state change. (In UML 2.0, this type of state machine is known as a behavioral state machine. There are also protocol state machines, which depict how an object can be used by specifying the conditions and states in which the object's various methods can be called.)

Statechart diagrams are closely related to activity diagrams. The main difference between the two is that statechart diagrams focus on an object's state, whereas activity diagrams focus on the flow of activities to be performed. Typically, you use a statechart diagram to model the discrete stages of an object's lifetime, whereas you use an activity diagram to model the sequence of activities in a process. So, what does this really mean? You generally use a statechart diagram to model objects and the transitions between objects, based on the system and software design. Quite often, the state transitions are time-based. Activity diagrams are more business-like, and people often use them to describe a flow of events for satisfying a business process. Chapter 2 provides detail on activity diagrams and their usage.

Each state in a statechart diagram represents a named condition or state that occurs during an object's lifetime that satisfies some condition or waits for some event to occur. A statechart diagram contains one start state and one or more end states. As with activity diagrams, statechart diagrams also can include decisions, synchronizations, and activities. [RATR1]

In the UML, you model a state as a rectangle with corners that are rounded off, as shown in Figure 8-1.

Figure 8-1   *UML state.*

A state's name can contain letters, numbers, and punctuation marks (except for a colon, which in the UML describes separation between an element's name and its type). It can consist of multiple lines of text. In addition, a state's name should be descriptive. For example, if your statechart diagram describes how an automobile transmission works, it would be appropriate to name the states First Gear, Second Gear, Reverse, and so forth.

States are connected using relationships called *transitions* and transition descriptions called *events*. An event can cause a transition from one state to another. In an "event/action" pair, the action describes what is done in response to an event. Figure 8-2 shows an example of what a partial statechart diagram for an automobile transmission might look like. The transitions are the lines with arrows as in those connecting the first gear to second gear states, and the descriptions on those transitions, Upshift and Downshift, are the events.

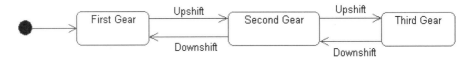

Figure 8-2   *Statechart diagram.*

As with an activity diagram, a statechart diagram contains a starting point, which begins the transition to a state. Unlike an activity diagram, a statechart diagram can contain several *substates* each with a starting point. A substate (or "nested state") is one state that is nested within another state.

You can nest states to any depth in a statechart diagram A nested state is a state that takes part in and is embedded as part of another state, but it cannot be achieved without first satisfying the enclosing states, which are referred to as superstates. Everything that lies within the bounds of a superstate is the state's content. Figure 8-3 shows a statechart diagram similar to the one in Figure 8-2. However, the statechart diagram in Figure 8-3 includes additional states, substates, and superstates using nesting. Forward and Reverse are substates nested within the state of Movement. You will also see a transition whose description reads "transition to self," which means exactly what it says—the state transitions to itself. In this example, the Movement state transitions from one direction to another (i.e., Forward and Reverse).

People usually use statechart diagrams to model real-time and embedded systems where architects and developers need to design the event-driven behavior of those systems. For instance, the telecom industry would use a statechart diagram for real-time embedded system development to show different switches reacting to network conditions. In such a scenario, the analyst or designer would need to determine timings, on and off activation, message sharing, and other events. If the developer didn't understand exactly when these events were to occur, he would find it difficult to develop software that could manage these systems, which require such precise actions.

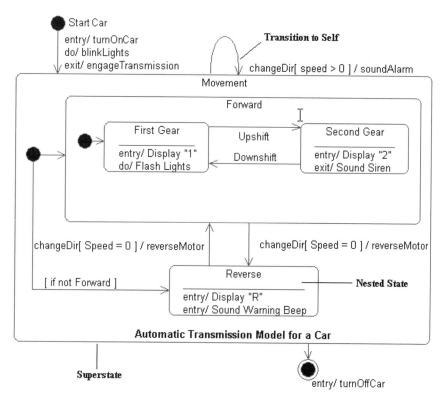

Figure 8-3 *Nesting states. [RATR2]*

Collaboration Diagrams

The UML contains two types of interaction diagrams. We discussed the first type, sequence diagrams, in Chapters 3, 4, and 7. The other type of interaction diagram is a *collaboration diagram.*

A collaboration diagram shows how objects interact and how they are organized. It also shows the links between those objects. Of all the diagrams in the UML, the collaboration diagram is one of the least complicated.

Figure 8-4 shows how the price of an order is calculated using the three basic elements of a collaboration diagram:

- Objects
- Links
- Messages (shown as text on a link)

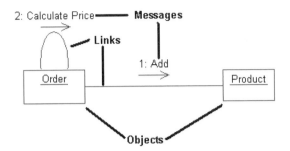

Figure 8-4 *Collaboration diagram.*

You can create multiple messages on one link, and each message is numbered based on the order in which it will be executed. Figure 8-4 demonstrates this by showing that a product is added to an order before the order price is calculated.

Object Diagrams

An *object diagram* is a snapshot of the objects within a system at a particular point in time. Because an object diagram shows instances instead of classes, people sometimes refer to it as an *instance diagram*. Unlike a class, which shows attributes to further describe itself, an object uses values for the attributes in its definition, such as describing the attribute of "phoneNumber" with actual numbers rather than just the attribute name of phoneNumber. Figure 8-5 shows an object diagram. [BOOCH1] (Note that an object "Joe" of class "Customer" is shown as "Joe:Customer".)

Although object diagrams aren't as popular as class diagrams, they do provide value to people who need to understand how the objects actually will exist when the software is executing. An object diagram helps the developer understand what type of data he can capture in the system because it defines not only the attributes, but also their values. Furthermore, a database team can understand the data, enabling them to determine data types as well as how to optimize for that data. You can more easily do validation with customers when you can point to not only the objects that are being created but also to expected data to be captured and their relationships. This provides a nice way to ensure you are building what the customer expects.

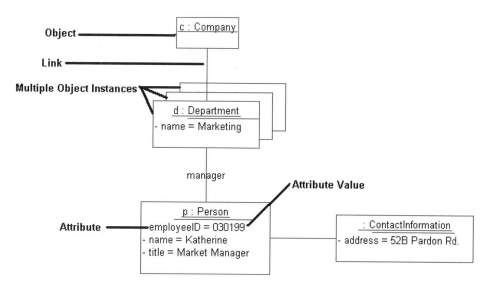

Figure 8-5 *Object diagram.*

More on UML 2.0

As of this writing, the Object Management Group (OMG) and its voting members are finalizing the latest specification of the UML, version 2.0. In Chapter 1, we discuss the history of the UML. Here, we discuss its future.

UML 2.0 has been long awaited by tools vendors, corporate users of the UML, and teachers because it has been in the works for several years. The emergence of real-time and embedded systems growth, web services, new languages (Java, C#, and so forth), notations to support systems engineering, and new business needs has necessitated a significant update to the language, which is nearly complete. The rest of this section describes what mere mortals can expect in version 2.0 and discusses how these changes benefit you.

Explaining the complete new version of the UML is beyond the scope of this book. We wrote this book to explain what you, as a mere mortal, need to know to use the UML to your advantage. Therefore, we are covering the key parts you are most likely to need to understand without going into excruciating and overwhelming detail. For additional resources on UML and UML 2.0, see Chapter 10, "Where Can I Learn More?."

Some additions to the UML in version 2.0 that we will discuss include updates to collaboration, activity, sequence, component, and class diagrams. Throughout this book, we have noted UML 2.0 changes to the various modeling constructs and diagrams. We will focus on the remaining important pieces that you will use most often as a modeler and mere mortal. Additional UML 2.0 features have been added, and we don't specifically cover them here. Many of the new features included in UML 2.0 are in the underlying infrastructures and not the actual modeling elements that mere mortals will be use. In Appendix C, "UML Diagrams and Elements," we provide examples of the UML diagrams including the UML 1.x and 2.0 examples.

Changes to Collaboration Diagrams

Figure 8-6 provides an overview of all the diagram types that will be available in UML 2.0 (see Chapter 1 for descriptions of each). Toward the bottom right of the figure, you can see what appears to be a new type of diagram: the communication diagram. This is not a new type of diagram. In version 2.0, collaboration diagrams are now called communication diagrams.

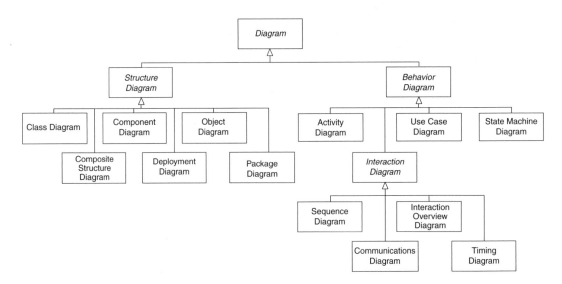

Figure 8-6   *UML diagrams and their structure. [OMG1]*

Change to Activity Diagrams

In Chapter 2, you read about activity diagrams and learned that activities are series of actions executed to provide a certain behavior. UML 2.0 changes the name of activities to *actions*. The meaning doesn't change, and they even still look the same. UML 2.0 still has activities, however now they contain actions and control nodes and are used to specify behavior.) Another such change affects swimlanes. They work in the same way and can be used both horizontally and vertically, but they are now called *partitions*. In addition, they now can be part of a bigger partition, as shown in Figure 8-7.

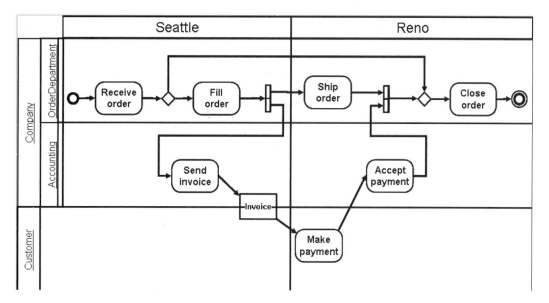

Figure 8-7   *Activity diagram partitions. [SELI1]*

In Figure 8-7, Reno and Seattle are vertical partitions, and Company is a horizontal partition with sub-partitions Accounting and Order Department. The other horizontal partition is Customer. The actions (activities in prior versions of UML) displayed inside of the partitions belong to that partition, which means the partition owner performs that action. For example, Receive Order is performed by the Company and within the Company by the Order Department. This provides you with added ability to qualify activity diagrams and to show how each action is achieved.

Changes to Sequence Diagrams

We agree with the many architects and developers who have said the changes to sequence diagrams are extremely important in the new specification because they will enable modelers to better express their software designs.

In former versions of the UML, sequence diagrams could not simply show alternate flows, especially common flows that you might want to reuse. UML version 2.0 has added new notations for this purpose. These new notations in sequence diagrams provide a "framed" approach to modeling, as you will read about later. (Frames are rectangles that enclose various sections of a diagram or interaction.) These changes enable sequence diagrams to show iterative, conditional, reference, and other behavior controls. UML 2.0 also enables modelers to express complete algorithms using sequence diagrams.

Figure 8-8 shows the use of interaction occurrences in a sequence diagram to provide you with the ability to understand and use the alternate flows within the software.

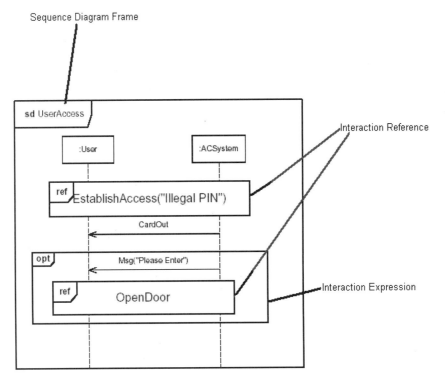

Figure 8-8 *Sequence diagram optional sequence modeling. [OMG2]*

Figure 8-8 describes the sequence of how a user is involved with using a room access system. It shows a referenced interaction occurrence (labeled "ref" in the upper-left corner) named EstablishAccess, which indicates that this portion of the interaction is defined elsewhere (in another diagram) and is "copied" here. This interaction occurrence would include the steps for the logic to read the access card, check the PIN, and if the PIN number is incorrect, display an illegal PIN message. If the access is successful, the optional interaction reference (labeled "opt" in the corner) is performed—the "Please Enter" message is displayed, and the door opens. These interaction frames makes complex sequences easier to create, reuse, and understand.

Changes to Component Diagrams

One of the difficulties in the prior version of the UML concerned modeling web services and other components that can contain multiple interfaces and that have logic contained in those interfaces. In UML 2.0, component visualization is enhanced. Whereas prior versions of the UML provided an icon for a component directly on the diagram, in version 2.0, the visualization difference appears in the upper-right corner (see Figure 8-9).

Figure 8-9   *New look for a component.*

Showing how components can be embedded within other components and how they interface internally within their parent components and externally to other components also is enhanced in version 2.0. With the new notation in this version, you can show the interfaces that a component requires and those it provides to other components. This new notation, illustrated in Figure 8-9, looks much like a "ball and socket." The ball fits into the socket and is provided visually in the notation. The ball indicates an interface that the component provides, and the socket indicates an interface that the component needs. When you put them together with another component, you complete the communication link between the components.

Figure 8-10 shows a component and the ball and socket as it pertains to a single component. Figure 8-11 shows how you would wire these components together using the new notation to create the Store component. In Figure 8-11, the Product component provides an interface (ball) named OrderableItem. The Order component requires (socket) the OrderableItem interface.

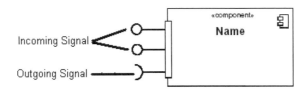

Figure 8-10   *Interfaces available from a component.*

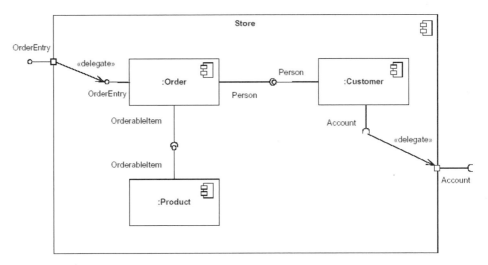

Figure 8-11   *Components wired together [OMG3].*

You can also see in Figure 8-11 two small squares on the outer edge of the Store component. Those squares are called *ports*, and they show an interaction point between the component and other external elements and also between the component and its internal parts. They serve to separate the component from its environment. All interactions with the component take place through its ports. The ball and socket icons attached to the ports show the interfaces that a component provides to or requires from its environment (respectively).

Changes to Class Diagrams

We discuss class diagrams in many chapters in this book—we first introduced them in Chapter 4, "Architectural Modeling," and then covered them in several chapters thereafter. For the mere mortal, there aren't a lot of relevant changes to class diagrams, but one that is important is structured classes. Structured classes provide the ability to hierarchically decompose a class into an internal structure. They enable a modeler to break down a complex object into its parts. Figure 8-12 shows that whenever an instance of the Car class is created, four instances of the Wheel class are created. In addition, one link each is created between the front wheel instances and the rear wheel instances.

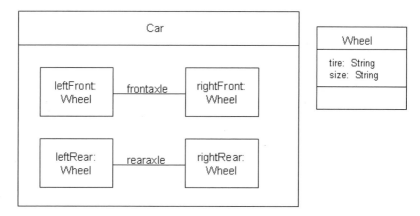

Figure 8-12   *Structured class.*

Ports and capsules are also used with class instances, just as we discussed in the previous section on component diagrams, to show how class instances are interfaced together in a structured class. Figure 8-13 shows a similar example to Figure 8-12, but adds in the wheel interfacing with the engine.

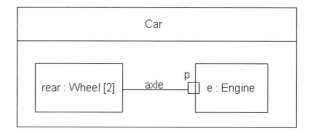

Figure 8-13   *Class instances with interfaces.*

UML version 2.0 also features numerous additional changes, including changes to the underlying structures and to the ways you capture metadata, but for mere mortals, and even for many expert modeling practitioners, the changes we highlight here and throughout this book will affect you most in your daily jobs.

Topics to Consider

You might want to examine these additional topics:

- If you are going to use the UML to its fullest, you might want to read other books on the topic and even take some classes that delve into ways you can model in the UML.
- Continue to monitor the Object Management Group web site (www.omg.org) as additional details regarding version 2.0 and subsequent changes become available. If you need a lengthy explanation of the UML specification, you can read it on the OMG web site.
- Although we touch on many object-oriented analysis and design (OOAD) concepts and discuss how to best understand and use the UML, understanding the concepts of OOAD is important to your continuing UML education and will enable you to correctly build UML models on your own.

Terms

Statechart diagram	Collaboration diagram
Object diagram	Sequence diagram
Activity diagram	Communication diagram
Instance	Port
Ball and socket	Object
Link	Message
UML 2.0	

Summary

In this chapter, we discussed diagrams that we did not cover in previous chapters and that are likely to be important to mere mortals. We covered models that help you understand what is happening in a system by looking at state and collaboration diagrams and what elements exist in a system by examining object diagrams.

We also took a peek into the future by discussing changes expected in the forthcoming UML 2.0 and how these changes will enable you to more effectively communicate your designs and understand how elements within your systems communicate with each other.

Review Questions

1. An object can do which of the following?
   a. Perform an activity
   b. Wait for an event
   c. Satisfy one or more conditions
   d. All of the above
   e. None of the above

2. Which type of system most often uses statechart diagrams?

3. An object uses what instead of attributes?
   a. Values
   b. Constructs
   c. Methods
   d. Operations

4. True or False: The next version of the UML is called UML 1.7.

5. UML 2.0 provides what visual notation for describing interfaces on a component?
   a. Pegs and holes
   b. Nuts and bolts
   c. Balls and sockets
   d. Stars and stripes

[BOOCH1] Booch, Grady, James Rumbaugh, and Ivar Jacobson. 1999. *The Unified Modeling Language User Guide.* Reading, MA: Addision-Wesley.

[OMG1] [OMG2] [OMG3] Object Management Group. 2004. *UML 2.0 Superstructure Specification.*

[RATR1] [RATR2] Rational Rose Version 2003 Help, IBM Rational Software.

[SELI1] Selic, Bran. 2003. *An Overview of UML 2.0.* Presentation at 2003 Rational Software User Conference.

How Do I Get Started Using the UML?

Topics Covered in This Chapter

Good Beginnings

    The Elephant

    Use Cases and Risk Management

    Recruits

Growing Your Own

    The Training Trap

    Mentors

    Apprenticeships

Working Together

    Modeling Teams

    The War Room

Topics to Consider

Terms

Summary

Review Questions

Introduction

This chapter is a bit different from the others in this book. Whereas the prior chapters answered multiple questions that we are frequently asked on the given topic, this chapter addresses one question: How do I get started with the UML? You've already made a good start by reading this book (and we are sure there will be many others in your future). But what's next? In this chapter, we will discuss various guidelines for adopting the UML. This is by no means an exhaustive treatment of how to fully prepare to utilize the UML. These are merely some key practices and common pitfalls, one or more of which will probably impact your UML journey, each in its own way. This chapter is meant to shine light on your path so that you can avoid at least these common problems and leverage hard-learned lessons from those who have gone before you.

Good Beginnings

Lao Tzu said, "A journey of a thousand miles must begin with a single step." However, if you are going a thousand miles, that first step better be in the right direction. The following topics will help you set your direction, decide your priorities, and choose good traveling companions.

The Elephant

Remember the old joke that asks, "How do you eat an elephant?" (answer: "One spoonful at a time.")? Just as that joke suggests, adopting the UML is not an all-or-nothing proposition. You do not have to know the entire UML to be able to use it. Remember, according to Booch, Rumbaugh, and Jacobson, "You can model 80 percent of most problems by using about 20 percent of the UML." [BOOCH1]

So, where do you start using UML on your projects? Given that you are not taking the full leap into UML for your entire project (which is a valid but challenging approach), one way is to adopt the UML based on need. Where do you need the most help? If your organization has difficulty satisfying or understanding your customer's needs, you can start by using use cases to work with those customers to elicit their requirements. If you need to redesign business processes, activity diagrams can help you understand the current processes and design the new ones. If your application developers and database developers don't communicate well, you can create your conceptual, logical, and physical database designs using UML. If you want to adapt UML incrementally, pick the area in which you have the greatest pain and use the UML to help improve that area. After you resolve that problem area, move on to the next, and so on—one spoonful at a time.

Use Cases and Risk Management

System and software development is inherently a risky business. Numerous studies over the years have reported what most of us have experienced—that most projects fail when measured against cost, capability, and/or schedule. One way to manage this risk is to drive your program with use cases.

After you define your use cases (for this exercise, having a good definition of each use case is sufficient—the detailed scenarios don't have to be fully defined yet), rank them based on how important they are and how difficult they will be to implement on a numeric scale of your choice; 1–10 is acceptable. Then plot the use cases as a scatter plot (see Figure 9-1).

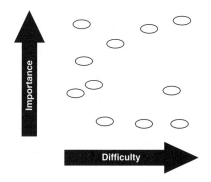

Figure 9-1   *Scatter plot of use cases.*

Next, partition this plot into four quadrants (see Figure 9-2).

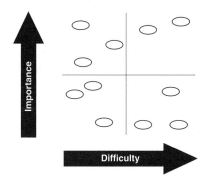

Figure 9-2   *Scatter plot quadrants.*

The upper-right quadrant (see Figure 9-3) displays the important but difficult use cases. These are your high-risk use cases. Develop these first because if you are unsuccessful with these, your project fails. Any other work you do on the unimportant use cases will be a waste of time and money.

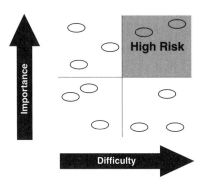

Figure 9-3 *Develop high-risk use cases first.*

The upper-left quadrant (see Figure 9-4) contains the use cases that are important but not as difficult as those in the upper-right quadrant. Of the remaining use cases, these provide the most value to your customer. Develop these next.

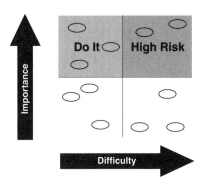

Figure 9-4 *Develop remaining important use cases next.*

The lower-left quadrant (see Figure 9-5) shows the use cases that are not as important but that also are not difficult to implement. If you have time and resources, develop these next.

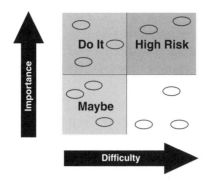

Figure 9-5   *Develop these easy use cases third.*

The lower-right quadrant (see Figure 9-6) contains the unimportant yet diffi-cult use cases. They provide little value for the effort you will expend. Do these last. If you get into a schedule or resource crunch, dump these first.

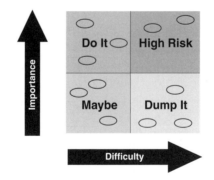

Figure 9-6   *Develop the remaining use cases last, if at all.*

Recruits

Even if you follow these tactics, your success still boils down to the people you pick to learn UML and OO techniques. Management often mistakenly assumes that programmers make the best OO designers. This is not necessar-ily true. You need two key skills to succeed in the OO arena: the ability to think in an abstract way (being able generalize specific ideas to a higher abstraction level in order to create resilient, flexible systems), and the ability to thoroughly analyze problems and synthesize solutions.

In our experience, in any random selection of candidates who might or might not possess these two skills, only 25 percent will immediately understand the concepts and value of OO analysis and design, and 33 percent won't understand it at all and most likely will reject UML/OO concepts outright. As for the remaining people, they will somewhat understand and accept the concepts. (This last group would particularly benefit from mentors so that they don't go down the wrong path with their designs; see the next section.)

Growing Your Own

If you plan to scale a face of Mount Kilimanjaro or Mount Everest, you certainly would want a well-trained team and some experts to guide your climb. This section helps you take those raw recruits you just selected and turn them into a well-prepared team.

The Training Trap

As you begin to take these first steps, though, don't fall into the training trap. We all get those glossy magazine-like advertisements from training companies that list dozens of classes you can take. I surveyed a few recently. Overall, about 85–90 percent of the courses listed were for programming languages. The promise is that you'll take the one-week course, and then you'll return to your cubicle and be able to start coding in the new programming language the next week. This promise is the bait in the trap. This might work for programming languages, but not for understanding how to perform analysis and design with the UML. (By way of analogy, building a bridge is different from designing the bridge, requiring different skills and tools.) A programming language might be object-oriented, but learning an object-oriented language does not mean you will learn the concepts for good object-oriented design using the UML. However, the industry has expected that training outcome for so long (based on programming-language course results) that they expect it for UML and object-oriented training courses, too.

From the Real World—Trapped!

I visited a company for a day-long series of job interviews. A bit past midday, I entered the office of the Vice President of Development. After exchanging pleasantries, we sat down, and she gave me a very odd look, though I thought it was just my imagination at first. I had been interviewing all day without a break, not stopping for lunch, and my energy level was flagging. Then she snapped at me, "So you're the object-oriented expert. I just sent my people to a C++ class. They came back and now they can't do this OO stuff. You tell me why." I thought to myself, "Whoa! I wasn't the trainer. How would I know?"

She had fallen into "the training trap." I explained to her that she had misplaced her expectations. C++ is a programming language. Language classes don't typically teach you how to do good object-oriented analysis and design (OOAD)—no more than learning the English language will enable you to write "The Great American Novel." She hadn't sent them to an OOAD class or a UML class. But the industry is used to sending people to a programming language class for a week and then back to work to begin coding in that language, which is the wrong expectation for UML and OOAD. If you go to a UML class, you might be able to learn the UML basics in a week. However, you need more if you want people who can do OOAD well (more on this later in this chapter). Plus, you need to ensure that real practitioners are providing the training, not just people who pitch canned training slides.

Her scowl didn't change. I finished the interview gauntlet later that day. And yes, I got the job.

Lessons Learned

1. Understanding an object-oriented programming language does not mean you understand the UML.
2. Understanding an object-oriented programming language does not mean you understand object-oriented analysis and design.
3. Expect the unexpected during interviews. ☺

Mentors

UML training classes can only take you so far. You also need training in OOAD. But even this only provides you with a foundation upon which to build your knowledge of the UML. To really develop the skills to perform excellent OOAD with UML, you need more. You need mentors to help guide your people through the intricacies. When starting out, you might have to hire mentors from outside your company. There are many consultancies where you can find such people. Make sure part of their job is to create in-house mentors for the future. In that way, you can seed new projects with your own in-house mentors. Then these internal people will groom additional mentors, and so forth. By repeating this process, you will develop internal expertise on UML and OO for your future projects and can reduce your dependency on external experts.

Apprenticeships

An activity closely related to mentoring is apprenticeship. Your external or internal mentor is not responsible only for helping train your up and coming UML specialists. Your newly minted UML/OO folks should not be thrown onto a real project alone—they should apprentice on a project with an experienced mentor. Projects in the real world have much more complex issues than you will ever see even in the best training regime. Training problems are structured and controlled in order to teach specific concepts and provide safe, no-risk learning. Not so on real projects.

Apprenticing will help your folks through the "Blank Sheet of Paper Syndrome" from which even your best newly trained OO folks are likely to suffer. This syndrome occurs when they are assigned to a new project and begin the task of modeling the system with that big, blank sheet of paper (or blank computer screen). Thoughts such as, "Where do I start?," or "This isn't like what we learned in class," or "What should I do?" immediately pop up. In the best case, this mentally paralysis doesn't last too long. In the worst case, these neophytes might start down the wrong path, and all their subsequent work can be for naught. You will also find that most people don't get over this syndrome until their third new OO project or so.

Working Together

We will wrap up this chapter by discussing teamwork guidelines for projects on the UML and object-oriented journey.

Modeling Teams

The old saying "too many cooks spoil the broth" is true for modeling. When you assemble teams to model your system, subsystem, or application (whatever level of abstraction you are working at), large teams can be disastrous.

Our experience shows that on a team with more than five people, progress will not be forthcoming. Because you can model a system in so many different ways, a large group of people might never agree on the representation of the systems.

On the other end of the spectrum, a modeling team needs to have a certain critical mass. At least one person on the team has to have business or domain expertise in the area in which you are working. For example, if you are building a system to support commodities trading, you need someone who is an expert in commodities trading. Also, at least two people on the team should have expertise in UML modeling. Why two? As we mentioned, you often can model a business or system in many ways. By having two expert modelers on your team, you can ensure balance. We have seen some modelers become so enamored with a particular modeling technique or pattern that they try to apply it to every problem they encounter. With a second modeler, you add another perspective, and the team will be more likely to come up with a better design. Plus, the team members can learn from each other's experiences, and both become better at their craft. In summary, a modeling team size of three to five is very effective.

As you begin working with your team, you might notice that the business expert will begin to understand some of the modeling concepts. As a result, he mistakenly might begin to assume he fully understands UML modeling and object-oriented techniques. Make sure you make it clear to everyone on the team that the modelers are responsible for modeling and the domain expert is responsible for explaining the "business" concepts that the modelers will depict.

The War Room

When multiple teams are working on the same project, it is very useful to create a "war room." This is a common area where all the teams post their models on the walls so that every team can see the state of every other team's designs at any time. A war room also provides a common meeting area where a team can work, surrounded by all of their models.

Togetherness is a wonderful thing. Although we recommend you create a war room for your project teams, you need to make sure the teams don't live in the war room and do *all* their modeling work together, *all* the time. We have seen such consensus modeling attempted; it is not effective for long and will cause the team to burn out quickly. Team members also need some time to themselves to work on their individual designs, to consider what they have learned from other team members, and to synthesize new ideas and concepts. Because modeling is a creative activity, your people will need some "quiet time" to be creative and then collaborative time with the other team members (in the war room) to exchange and review their designs.

Also, regarding collaboration, when you do establish a group of mentors in your organization, you should utilize them to review your designs periodically. This is particularly valuable when you are approaching an important design review. Your project benefits from their experience, and they benefit by gaining new knowledge about yet another project that they can use as they mentor others.

Topics to Consider

You might want to examine these additional topics:

- If you were developing a training curriculum, in what order would you provide UML, programming language, and object-oriented analysis and design training classes?
- In the early, pre-design phases of projects, the UML models will change a great deal. How would you convince management that progress is really being made? What would you use as evidence?

Terms

Mentors	Apprenticeship
Elephant	Object-oriented analysis and design
War Room	Risk management

Summary

We began this chapter by easing the trepidation many people have for the UML. Although the UML can be complex, you learned that in order to get started, you need to learn only about 20 percent of the UML to do most of your modeling. We then discussed some of the pitfalls concerning training and what you need to know to do UML modeling beyond the UML language itself.

Next, we expressed the roles that people should play in the learning process. We explained that you need experienced trainers and mentors who will guide the apprenticeship of your students. You also learned about the characteristics to look for in candidate students.

We wrapped up the chapter with a discussion about working together in small teams and facilities that can help both creativity and collaboration.

Review Questions

1. True or False: The best way for people to get up to speed on the UML and OO development is to take a training class and then be assigned to a project to "fly solo."

2. Which use cases should be implemented first? Those that are:

   a. Important and easy

   b. Unimportant and difficult

   c. Important and difficult

   d. Unimportant and easy

3. When your modeling team exceeds 20 members, you should:

   a. Partition your war room into two sections

   b. Partition your war room into two to five sections

   c. Not partition your war room

4. True or False: Save your high-priced mentors for your critical OO projects.

5. How do you eat an elephant?

[BOOCH1] Booch, Grady, James Rumbaugh, and Ivar Jacobson. 1998. *The Unified Modeling Language User Guide*. Reading, MA: Addison-Wesley.

10

Where Can I Learn More?

Topics Covered in This Chapter

Resources for finding more information on:

UML

Object-Oriented Analysis and Design

Patterns

Enterprise Architectures and Frameworks

Introduction

This chapter is more of a listing of additional resources than a typical chapter. In this chapter, you will discover different books, web sites, articles, and more on UML and on other related topics discussed throughout this book. It will be organized a little differently as well. The subjects will be listed by topic and then resources about that topic directly beneath it. Undoubtedly, this chapter will not cover the thousands of resources that are available, but these are some key ones that have been particularly useful to ourselves and others in the past. Also, you can check the references at the end of each chapter for additional resources.

UML

Ambler, Scott. 2002. *The Elements of UML Style*. Cambridge University Press.

Booch, Grady, James Rumbaugh, and Ivar Jacobson. 1999. *The Unified Modeling Language User Guide*. Reading, MA: Addison-Wesley.

Fowler, Martin. 2003. *UML Distilled: A Brief Guide to the Standard Object Modeling Language*, Third Edition. Boston, MA: Addison-Wesley.

Naiburg, Eric and Robert Maksimchuk. 2001. *UML for Database Design*. Boston, MA: Addison-Wesley.

Object Modeling Group (OMG): www.omg.org.

Our web site: http://www.UMLForMereMortals.com.

Pender, Thomas. 2002. *UML Weekend Crash Course*. John Wiley & Sons.

Quatrani, Terry. 2000. *Visual Modeling with Rational Rose 2000 and UML*. Boston, MA: Addison-Wesley.

Rumbaugh, James, Ivar Jacobson, and Grady Booch. 2005. *The Unified Modeling Language Reference Manual*, Second Edition. Boston, MA: Addison-Wesley.

Scott, Kendall. 2001. *UML Explained*. Boston, MA: Addison-Wesley.

UML Resource Center: http://www-306.ibm.com/software/rational/uml/.

Object-Oriented Analysis and Design

Ambler, Scott and Barry McGibbon, ed. 2001. *The Object Primer*. Cambridge University Press.

Booch, Grady. 1994. *Object-Oriented Analysis and Design with Applications*, Second Edition. Reading, MA: Addison-Wesley.

Jacobson, Ivar. 1992. *Object-Oriented Software Engineering—A Use Case Driven Approach*. Reading, MA: Addison-Wesley.

Rumbaugh, Blaha, Premerlani, Eddy, and Lorensen. 1991. *Object-Oriented Modeling and Design*. Englewood Cliffs, NJ: Prentice Hall.

Patterns

Alur, Deepak, Dan Malks, and John Crupi. 2003. *Core J2EE Patterns, Second Edition: Best Practices and Design Strategies*. Upper Saddle River, NJ: Prentice Hall PTR.

Fowler, Martin. 1997. *Analysis Patterns: Reusable Object Models.* Reading, MA: Addison-Wesley.

Gamma, Erich, Richard Helm, Ralph Johnson, and John Vlissides. 1995. *Design Patterns: Elements of Reusable Object-Oriented Software.* Reading, MA: Addison-Wesley.

Larman, Craig. 2001. *Applying UML and Patterns: An Introduction to Object-Oriented Analysis and Design and the Unified Process.* Upper Saddle River, NJ: Prentice Hall PTR.

Enterprise Architectures and Frameworks

Enterprise Architect Magazine and web site: http://www.ftponline.com/ea/.

The Zachman Institute for Framework Advancement web site: www.zifa.com.

United States Treasury Department TEAF web site: http://www.treas.gov/teaf/arch_framework.doc.

A

Glossary

This glossary presents terms in "Mere Mortals" fashion. More formal definitions can be found in the various references cited in this book. Terms in **bold**, used in a definition, are defined elsewhere in the glossary.

abstraction—A representation that focuses on certain aspects of a thing and that might eliminate other aspects.

action—A processing step (an atomic behavior) taken as part an **activity**.

activity—A series of **actions** executed to provide a certain behavior.

activity diagram—A diagram that shows the flow of activities related to various **actors**.

actor—A role that a person, system, or other entity plays when interacting with the system being developed. Actors are external to the system.

aggregate—The class in an **aggregation** that represents the "whole" in the "whole-part" **relationship**.

aggregation—An **association** that represents a "whole-part" **relationship** between an **aggregate** and its parts.

analysis—A phase in the development lifecycle where you consider the requirements and determine *what* needs to be done to satisfy those requirements, not *how* they are to be satisfied.

argument—The value of a parameter of an **operation**.

association—A **relationship** between **classes**.

association class—A **class** that also has properties of an **association**.

attribute—Part of a **class** that describes or captures some property of that **class**.

cardinality—The number of things in a set.

child (a.k.a. **subclass**)—A specialization of the **parent** (a.k.a. **superclass**) in a **generalization** relationship.

class—An element that describes a group of objects that have the same **attributes**, **operations**, **relationships**, **constraints**, and meaning.

class diagram—A diagram that provides a static **view** of the system.

collaboration—The cooperative behavior of a group of elements.

collaboration diagram—See **communication diagram**.

communication diagram—A type of **interaction diagram** that focuses on the relationships between the **objects** that participate in an **interaction**.

component—A replaceable physical part in a system that provides a specified set of **interfaces** and capabilities.

component diagram—A diagram that shows the relationships between **components**.

composite—A class that is related to one or more classes (a.k.a. the parts) by a **composition** relationship. The composite is responsible for the creation and destruction of the parts.

composite aggregation—A tighter, more intimate form of **aggregation** where the "parts" cannot exist without the "whole" (a.k.a. the **composite**). In a composition, a part can only be included in one **composite** at a time.

composition—See **composite aggregation.**

constraint—A restriction on a model element.

delegation—The capability of an **object** to send a message to a second **object**, typically for the purpose of having the second **object** perform a function for the originating **object**.

dependency—A relationship between two modeling elements in which a change to the independent element affects the dependent element.

deployment diagram—A diagram that shows the runtime configuration of a system.

design—A phase in the development lifecycle where you focus on *how* the system will be built to meet its requirements.

domain—A body of knowledge that has a commonly understood set of terms, concepts, and techniques used by the people working in that area.

encapsulation—A concept whereby an **class's** data is hidden from outside entities and can only be accessed by external entities through the **operations** provided by that **class**.

event—Something that occurs that can trigger a **transition** in a **statechart diagram**.

extend—A **relationship** between an extending **use case** to a base **use case**, typically showing how the extending **use case** can change the behavior of the base **use case** under certain conditions.

focus of control—A rectangular bar on a **lifeline** in a **sequence diagram** that shows the period of time during which an **object** is performing an action (i.e., has the "thread of control").

generalization—A **relationship** between elements where the **child** elements are specialized versions of their **parent** element and can inherit the structure and behavior of their **parent**.

guard condition—A condition that, when satisfied, enables a **transition** to execute.

include—A relationship between a base **use case** to an inclusion **use case**, showing how the base **use case** includes the behavior of the inclusion **use case**.

inheritance—The mechanism in a **generalization** that enables the more specialized elements to inherit the structure and behavior of the more general element.

instance—A unique occurrence of an abstract element (e.g., an **object** instance of a **class**).

interaction—The specification of how messages flow among a group of **objects** for a given purpose.

interaction diagram—The name for a set of diagrams that depict the dynamic behavior of a set of **objects**. These include **communication diagrams**, **sequence diagrams**, and **interaction overview diagrams**.

interaction overview diagram—A type of high-level **activity diagram** that depicts an overview of the control flow of an **interaction**.

interface—A set of **operations** that specify the services provided by an element.

lifeline—A line that represents the existence, over time, of an individual element in an **interaction**.

message—A communication between **objects**.

meta-model—A model that is built to describe a model.

method—The detailed implementation of an **operation**.

multiple inheritance—A situation where a **subclass** inherits from more than one **superclass**.

multiplicity—The specification of the allowed cardinalities on an end of an **association**.

n-ary association—An **association** between three or more **classes**.

object—An **instance** of a **class**.

object diagram—A diagram that shows **objects** and their relationships at a given point in time.

operation—A service provided by a **class**.

package—A general mechanism for gathering model elements into groups.

package diagram—A diagram that depicts the dependencies between packages.

parameter—The specification of an **argument**.

parent (a.k.a. **superclass**)—A **generalization** of the **child** (a.k.a. **subclass**) in a **generalization** relationship.

polymorphism—The ability of a child class to override (and thus redefine) the **operations** of its parent class.

postcondition—A condition that must be true after an operation is completed.

precondition—A condition that must be true when an operation is executed.

profile—A set of model elements that have been customized (using standard UML extension mechanisms) for a specific purpose.

qualifier—An **association** attribute that partitions a set of **objects** on one side of an **association**.

realization—The implementation of something specified by another model element (e.g., a **use case realization** implements a **use case**).

relationship—A general term denoting a connection between model elements (e.g., **association**, **composition**, **generalization**).

role—A specific set of behaviors of a given model element.

sequence diagram—A type of **interaction diagram** that focuses on the messages passed between **objects** in time order.

signature—An **operation's** name and **parameters**.

single inheritance—A situation where a **subclass** inherits from one **superclass**.

state—The condition of an **object** at a point in time.

state machine diagram (a.k.a statechart diagram)—A diagram that depicts the **states** of an **object** and its **transitions** between those states over the object's lifetime.

stereotype—A standard UML mechanism used to extend existing UML elements for specific purposes.

subclass (a.k.a. **child**)—A specialization of the **superclass** (a.k.a. **parent**) in a **generalization relationship**.

superclass (a.k.a. **parent**)—A **generalization** of the **subclass** (a.k.a. **child**) in a **generalization relationship**.

swimlane—A partitioning of elements in an **activity diagram**.

tagged value—A standard extension mechanism of the UML where a property of an element is defined as a name-value pair.

timing diagram—A diagram that depicts changes in **state** or condition of a **lifeline** (typically an **object**) with a focus on the timing of events.

transition—A **relationship** between two **states** that depicts how an object will change **state**.

trigger—An event that causes an **object** to change **state**.

use case—A series of transactions performed between the system and an **actor** that yields valuable results to the **actor**.

use case diagram—A diagram that depicts the **relationships** between the **actors** and the system's **use cases**.

view—A depiction of certain aspects of a model, which addresses the particular viewer's interests or concerns.

visibility—The specification of how or whether a model element can be seen by other elements.

B

Answers to Review Questions

Chapter 1   Introduction to the UML

1. What does the acronym "UML" stand for?

   Answer: The Unified Modeling Language

2. Who controls the UML standard?

   Answer: The Object Management Group (OMG)

3. True or False: The UML is a proprietary standard.

   Answer: False

4. What type of systems can you model with the UML?

   Answer: Any

5. True or False: You can use the UML only for object-oriented development.

   Answer: False

6. What methodology do you use when you use the UML?

   Answer: Any. The UML is methodology agnostic.

7. Name three benefits to modeling with the UML.

   Answer: There are more than three. Three typical benefits are:

   a. The UML can reduce misunderstandings (and therefore errors) by providing a common language all stakeholders can use to communicate clearly.

   b. The UML is a non-proprietary, standards-based language. Thus, it has worldwide acceptance, is being taught in universities, and has support from many software vendors.

   c. While being a standard, the UML also is extensible.

8. Does a model have to be visual?

    Answer: No, a model can be textual, visual, mathematical, and more.

9. What is analysis paralysis?

    Answer: Analysis paralysis is when you spend too much time analyzing a problem and take too long to become productive. This often happens early in the development process, especially if delivery iterations are unclear or not well defined.

10. True or False: UML models are of value to even small projects of one or two developers.

    Answer: True. Understanding the architecture and business helps to ensure you are building the right thing, and it provides a visualization of what you are going to build, exposing potential design risks before you spend the time to implement the system.

11. Name two ways to model a business.

    Answer: "as-is" and "to-be"

12. What is the most commonly used UML diagram?

    Answer: Class diagram

13. What UML diagram do you use to model workflow?

    Answer: Activity diagram

14. What diagram type do business analysts most commonly use to identify high-level business processes?

    Answer: Use case diagram

Chapter 2   Business Models

1. When is it recommended to not model the business as it currently exists and to model the business only as you want it to be in the future?

    Answer: That approach is *not* recommended. You always should model your business as it exists.

2. Name two situations where you should model your entire business.

   Answer: There are more than two such situations. Two are:

   a. If you have an overarching objective that will transform most or all of your business.

   b. If you have a project or set of interrelated projects that will take a long time (years) to implement.

3. What is the purpose of the business analysis model?

   Answer: To show how your business operates internally to provide the services the business actors want.

4. True or False: Activity diagrams show the time-ordered sequence of message flows between the elements in your model.

   Answer: False

5. The business use case diagram:

   a. Shows the business workflow

   b. Shows the configuration of your business's hardware

   c. Shows how your business internally satisfies your customers' requests

   d. Shows the context of your business

   Answer: d. Shows the context of your business

6. Name three areas where business modeling can improve your business.

   Answer: There are more than three. Three examples are:

   a. Discover and eliminate redundant processes

   b. Find and resolve incorrect or conflicting business rules

   c. Identify potential areas for consolidation, efficiencies, or other improvements

Chapter 3   Requirements Modeling

1. True or False: Changes in requirements are expected and do not significantly impact the success of projects.

   Answer: False

2. True or False: The cost to repair defects increases linearly over the lifecycle of a project.

   Answer: False

3. "The system shall provide redundant backup of all data" is a:

   a. Nonfunctional requirement

   b. Functional requirement

   c. Combination of a.) and b.)

   d. None of the above

   Answer: b. Functional requirement

4. When discussing the domain of laundering your clothes, would the following be good use cases? If not, give at least one reason why not.

   a. Add Detergent   **Answer:** No, it is not a complete flow.

   b. Wash Clothes   **Answer:** Yes.

   c. Agitate Laundry   **Answer:** No, it is not actor focused.

5. Actors can:

   a. Depict a single role

   b. Depict multiple roles

   c. Not depict any roles

   d. All of the above

   e. Both a.) and b.)

   f. None of the above

   Answer: d. All of the above. Some might answer "Both a.) and b.)," which would be usually correct. However, when you consider that events can be actors (e.g., time, change in monetary policy), "All of the above" is appropriate.

6. True or False: An included use case inserts its flow at a single point in the base use case.

   Answer: True

7. True or False: The flow of an extending use case must always be executed.

   Answer: False. It is executed if the triggering condition is true.

8. True or False: The flow of a base use case is complete even without any of its possible extending use cases.

   Answer: True

Chapter 4   Architectural Modeling

1. What elements are contained in the three compartments in a class?

   Answer: Class name, attributes, and operations

2. Which of the following is not an architectural framework?

   a. Zachman Framework

   b. Federal Enterprise Architecture Framework

   c. Rational Architecture Framework

   d. Department of Defense Architecture Framework

   Answer: c. Rational Architecture Framework

3. True or False: Boolean is a standard UML attribute type that has two options, yes or no.

   Answer: True

4. What geometric shape is used to visually describe an <<interface>>?

   Answer: Circle

5. True or False: MDA stands for Model Driven Assets.

   Answer: False. MDA stands for Model Driven Architecture.

Chapter 5   Application Modeling

1. True or False: Polymorphism is the concept that states a class's data is hidden from outside entities and can only be accessed by external entities through the operations provided by that class.

   Answer: False

2. What restriction does a rolename apply to a class?

   Answer: Rolenames partition the behavior(s) a class presents in an association with another class.

3. A qualifier selects specific object instances of the class:

   a. On the end of the association nearest to the qualifier

   b. On the far end of the association

   Answer: b. On the far end of the association

4. True or False: In an aggregation, when the "whole" is destroyed, all the parts are not necessarily destroyed.

   Answer: True. When you have a *composition* (or a *composite aggregation*), the parts are destroyed with the whole.

5. Which of the following are not a type of visibility:

   a. Private

   b. Partial

   c. Virtual

   d. Public

   e. Abstract

   f. Package

   g. Protected

   Answer: b. Partial, **c.** Virtual, and **e.** Abstract

Chapter 6 Database Modeling

1. Which one isn't a way to model databases?

   a. UML

   b. IDEF1X

   c. PBC

   d. IE

   Answer: c. PBC

2. What type of model describes the conceptual data model?

   Answer: Business analysis model

3. True or False: A class is stereotyped as <<entity>> in the logical data model.

   Answer: True

4. True or False: A class is stereotyped as <<trigger>> in the physical data model.

   Answer: False

5. Name three types of stereotypes used on a class during database design.

   Answer: Entity, business object, table

Chapter 7 Testing

1. Whether the scope of a test comprises system, integration, or subsystem testing is primarily determined by:

   a. The number of use cases involved in the test

   b. The number of classes involved in the test

   c. The number of subsystems involved in the test

   d. The number of UML diagrams involved in the test

   Answer: c. The number of subsystems involved in the test

2. True or False: Detailed algorithmic processing can best be represented in a class diagram.

   Answer: False. Activity diagrams are suited for this purpose.

3. Testing that focuses on the internals of the component under test is known as:

   a. White box testing

   b. Regression testing

   c. Black box testing

   d. Non-functional testing

   e. Performance testing

   Answer: a. white box testing

4. The UML diagrams that can show how your test procedures should flow are:

   a. Statechart diagrams

   b. Activity diagrams

   c. Sequence diagrams

   d. a and b

   e. b and c

   f. a, b, and c

   g. None of the above

   Answer: f. a, b, and c

5. True or False: Test personnel should become involved in the systems development after the detailed analysis and design models are complete.

   Answer: False. They should be involved as early as possible.

6. Name a type of non-functional testing that can be aided by UML diagrams.

   Answer: Performance testing

Chapter 8   Is That All There Is?

1. An object can do which of the following?

   a. Perform an activity

   b. Wait for an event

   c. Satisfy one or more conditions

   d. All of the above

   e. None of the above

   Answer: d. All of the above

2. Which type of system most often uses statechart diagrams?

   Answer: Real-time and embedded systems

3. An object uses what instead of attributes?

   a. Values

   b. Constructs

   c. Methods

   d. Operations

   Answer: a. Values

4. True or False: The next version of the UML is called UML 1.7.

   Answer: False. It is UML 2.0.

5. UML 2.0 provides what visual notation for describing interfaces on a component?

   a. Pegs and holes

   b. Nuts and bolts

   c. Balls and sockets

   d. Stars and stripes

   Answer: c. Balls and sockets

Chapter 9   How Do I Get Started Using the UML?

1. True or False: The best way for people to get up to speed on the UML and OO development is to take a training class and then be assigned to a project to "fly solo."

   Answer: False. Newly trained people should apprentice on a project, guided by an experienced mentor.

2. Which use cases should be implemented first? Those that are:

   a. Important and easy

   b. Unimportant and difficult

   c. Important and difficult

   d. Unimportant and easy

   Answer: c. Important and difficult

3. When your modeling team exceeds 20 members, you should:

   a. Partition your war room into two sections

   b. Partition your war room into two to five sections

   c. Not partition your war room

   Answer: Trick question. You should not have 20 members on a given modeling team.

4. True or False: Save your high-priced mentors for your critical OO projects.

   Answer: False

5. How do you eat an elephant?

   Answer: One spoonful at a time.

C

UML Diagrams and Elements

This appendix provides examples of many of the UML diagrams, but does not include all diagrams available.

Globally Used Elements

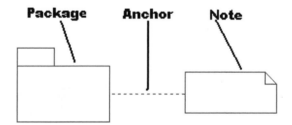

Figure C-1 *Modeling elements used in many diagrams.*

Use Case Diagram

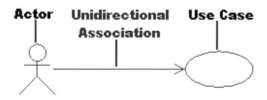

Figure C-2 *Use case, actor, and association.*

Activity Diagram

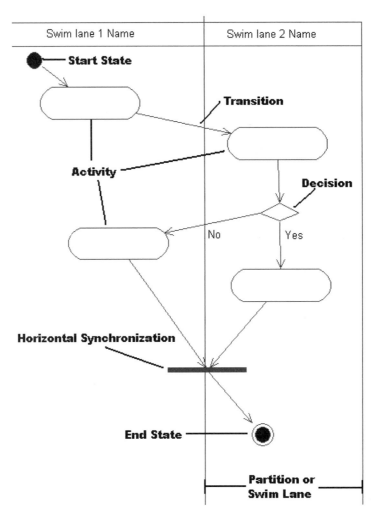

Figure C-3 *Activity diagram.*

Sequence Diagram

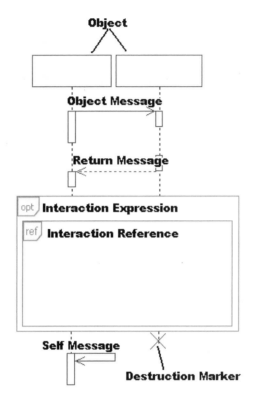

Figure C-4   *Basic sequence diagram.*

Collaboration (UML 1.x) or Communication (UML 2.0) Diagram

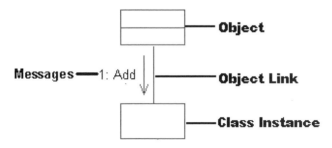

Figure C-5   *Collaboration diagram.*

Class Diagram

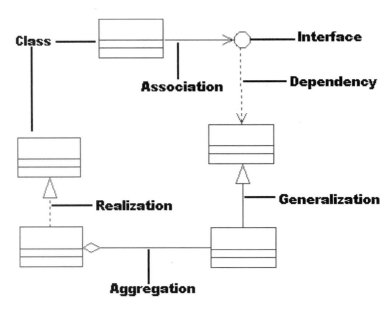

Figure C-6 *Class diagram.*

Component Diagram

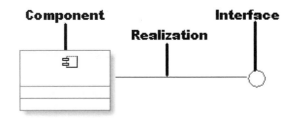

Figure C-7 *Component diagram.*

Deployment Diagram

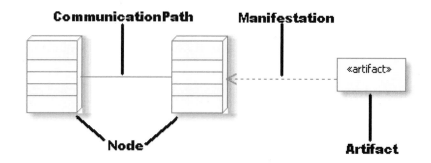

Figure C-8   *Deployment diagram.*

Statechart Diagram

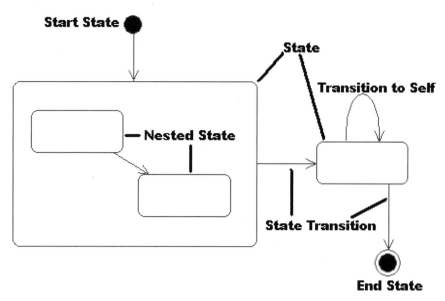

Figure C-9   *Statechart diagram.*

Timing Diagram

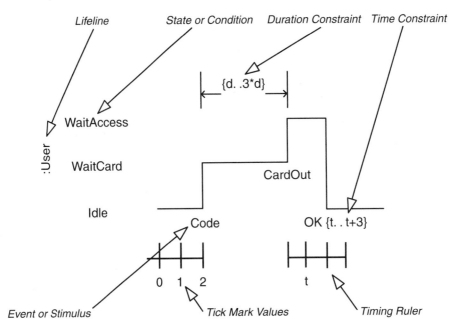

Figure C-10 *Timing diagram. [OMG1]*

[OMG1] Object Management Group. 2004. UML 2.0 Superstructure Specification.

Index

Symbols

"25 rule," 46

A

abstraction, 72
activity diagrams, 16
  alternative flows, 44
  Business Use Case Model, 38-42, 44
  database modeling, 146, 148
  in UML 2.0, 195
  synchronization points, 42
activity models, database modeling,
    146, 148
actors
  business actors, 34
  use cases, 72-75
aggregation, 48
  class diagrams, 129-130
algorithmic testing, 178-179
alternate flows, 81
  activity diagrams, 44
analysis models, 177
  unit, class, and algorithmic testing,
    178-179
analysis paralysis, 9
applications
  modeling, 120
    class diagrams, 121-130

class diagrams. See class
    diagrams, 131
  examples, 114-115, 118-119
  how deeply to model, 119-120
  sequence diagrams, 133-135
  reasons for modeling, 114-117
apprenticeships, 210
architectural patterns, 106-107
architecture, 90
  enterprise architecture, 92-93
  logical architecture, 94-95
    class diagrams, 95-99
    systems and subsystems, 99-100
  MDA (model driven architecture),
    108-109
  physical architecture, 101
    component diagrams, 102
    deployment diagrams, 103-104
    operations, 101-102
    stereotypes, 104
  reasons for modeling, 91-92
  software architecture, 94
  system architecture, 93-94
association classes, class diagrams,
    131-132
associations, class diagrams, 127-129
asynchronous messages, 84

B

basic flow, 81
behavior diagrams, 16
black box testing, 169
"Blues Brothers," 26
Booch method, 2
Booch, Grady, 2
BPML (Business Process Modeling
    Language), 18
business actors, 34
Business Analysis Model, 46-48, 50
  sequence diagrams, 50-51, 53-54
business analysis models
  conceptual models, 150-151
  testing, 173-176
business entities, conceptual models, 150
business models, 23-26
  Business Analysis Model, 46-48, 50
    sequence diagrams, 50-51, 53-54
  examples, 27-33
  reasons for modeling, 26-29
  reasons for modeling entire businesses,
    31-32
  UML, 33-35
business objects diagrams, 48
Business Process Modeling Language
    (BPML), 18
business rules, examples, 45
business use case diagram, 35-38
Business Use Case Model, 35
  activity diagrams, 38-42, 44
  business use case diagram, 35-38
business use case models, testing,
    168-173
business use cases, 35

C

cardinality, 142
CBD (Component-Based Development),
    4, 102
characteristics of use cases, 65-70
choosing designers, 207-208
class diagrams, 15, 95-97, 99
  application modeling, 121
    aggregation and composition,
      129-130
    association classes, 131-132
    associations, 127-129
    classes, 121-124
    constraints, 132
    generalization, 130
    operations, 124-126
  database modeling, 148-149, 154,
    156-158
  in UML 2.0, 199-200
class models, database modeling, 148-149
class testing, 178-179
classes, 122
  class diagrams, 121-124
collaboration diagrams, 16, 191-192
  in UML 2.0, 194
component diagrams, 15, 102
  in UML 2.0, 197-198
Component-Based Development (CBD),
    4, 102
composite structure diagrams, 16
composition, class diagrams, 129-130
conceptual models
  database modeling, 149
    business analysis models, 150-151
  defining, 151-152
  examples, 152

constraints, class diagrams, 132
containment, 49
context diagrams, 36
Core J2EE Patterns, 107
Covey, Stephen, 166

D

DAO pattern, 107
database design, 139-140
  notations, 140-142
database modeling
  examples, 143-144
  UML, 142-144, 149
    activity models, 146-148
    class models, 148-149
    conceptual models, 149-152
    logical models, 153-158
    physical models, 158-160
    use case models, 145-146
database transactions, 177
databases
  modeling. *See* database modeling
  testing, 177
deployment diagrams, 15, 103-104
descriptions, use case descriptions, 81-82
design models, 177
  unit, class, and algorithmic testing,
    178-179
designers
  apprenticeships, 210
  choosing, 207-208
  mentors, 209
  training traps, 208-209
designing databases, 139-140
  notations, 140-142
desirements, 60

destruction markers, 85
diagrams, 15-17, 188
  activity diagrams, 16
    alternative flows, 44
    Business Use Case Model, 38-42, 44
    database modeling, 146, 148
    in UML 2.0, 195
    synchronization points, 42
  behavior diagrams, 16
  business objects diagrams, 48
  business use case diagram, 35-38
  class diagrams, 15, 95-97, 99, 121
    aggregation and composition,
      129-130
    association classes, 131-132
    associations, 127-129
    classes, 121-124
    constraints, 132
    database modeling, 148-149, 154,
      156-158
    generalization, 130
    in UML 2.0, 199-200
    operations, 124-126
  collaboration diagrams, 16, 191-192
    in UML 2.0, 194
  component diagrams, 15, 102
    in UML 2.0, 197-198
  composite structure diagrams, 16
  deployment diagrams, 15, 103-104
  instance diagrams, 192
  interaction diagrams, 80
  interaction overview diagrams, 17
  object diagrams, 15, 192
  package diagrams, 16
  sequence diagrams, 16, 80, 83-85,
    133-135

Business Analysis Model, 50-51, 53-54
    in UML 2.0, 196-197
  statechart diagrams, 16, 188-190
  timing diagrams, 17
  use case diagrams, 16
  versus models, 17
domain classes, 121
domain entities, 177

E

enterprise architecture, 92-93
events, 189
examples
  "25 rule," 46
  business models, 27-33
  business rules, 45
  business use case diagrams, 36-37
  changing things without talking to
      real users, 70
  conceptual models, 152
  database modeling, 143-144
  for application modeling, 118-119
  of application modeling, 114-115
  of enterprise architecture, 92
  of requirements, 60
  of training traps, 208-209
  of use case creation, 82
  sequence diagrams, Business Analysis
      Model, 52-53
  testing, 166-167
extend relationship, 77
extension points, 80
Extreme Programming (XP), 14

F

FEAF (Federal Enterprise Architecture
    Framework), 92-93
flows
  alternative flows, 81
    activity diagrams, 44
  basic flow, 81
focus of control bar, 84
functional requirements, 63

G-H

generalization, class diagrams, 130
GPS (Global Positioning System), 65

I

IDEF1X (Integration Definition for
    Information Modeling), 140
include relationship, 76
inclusion points, 80
inheritance, 130
instance diagrams, 15, 192
Integration Definition for Information
    Modeling (IDEF1X), 140
integration tests, 169
  business analysis models, 174
interaction diagrams, 50, 80
interaction overview diagrams, 17

J

Jacobson, Ivar, 2

K

Kossiakoff, Alexander, 166

L

languages, programming languages, 119
lifelines, 51, 83
logical architecture, 94-95
  class diagrams, 95-99
  systems and subsystems, 99-100
logical models, database modeling, 153
  class diagrams, 154, 156-158

M

MDA (model driven architecture),
      108-109
mentors, 209
meta-models, 18
methodologies, 5
model driven architecture (MDA),
      108-109
modeling
  applications, 120
    class diagrams. *See* class diagrams
    examples, 114-115, 118-119
    how deeply to model, 119-120
    sequence diagrams, 133-135
    reasons for, 114-117
  architecture, reasons for, 91-92
  beware of what you are modeling, 49
  database modeling. *See* database
        modeling
  databases, database design, 139-140
  requirements, 64
    system use cases, 65
    use cases, 64
modeling teams, 210-211
models, 6-8

business models, 23
  Business Analysis Model, 46-48, 50
  examples, 27-33
  reasons for modeling, 26-29
  reasons for modeling entire
        businesses, 31-32
  UML, 33-35
comparing houses to software, 8-9
meta-models, 18
reasons for building, 8-9
versus diagrams, 17
what you can model with UML, 12-13
who should build models, 13-14
multiplicity, 50, 142

N

nesting states, 190
non-functional testing, 181
nonfunctional requirements, 63
notations, 140-142

O

object diagrams, 15, 192
Object Modeling Technique (OMT), 2
object-oriented development, 4
Object-Oriented Software Engineering
      method, 2
Objectory Method, 2
objects, 121-122, 188
OMT (Object Modeling Technique), 2
operations
  class diagrams, 124-126
  physical architecture, 101-102
ownership, 132

P

package diagrams, 16
patterns
　architectural patterns, 106-107
　DAO, 107
performance requirements, 181
performance testing, 181
physical architecture, 101
　component diagrams, 102
　deployment diagrams, 103-104
　operations, 101-102
　stereotypes, 104
physical data models, 160
physical models, database modeling, 158
　physical data models, 160
　physical versus logical, 158-159
polymorphism, 122, 126
ports, 198
post-conditions, 80
pre-conditions, 80
programming languages, 119
proprietary, UML, 3-4

Q

qualifiers, 128

R

Rational Software, 2
reasons
　for building models, 8-9
　for modeling applications, 114-117
　for modeling architecture, 91-92
　for modeling businesses, 26-27, 29
　for modeling entire businesses, 31-32
　for modeling with UML, 10-11
　for using requirements, 62-63
regression testing, 181

relationships, 131
　extend, 77
　include, 76
　use cases, 75-79
requirements, 59-61
　examples of, 60
　functional requirements, 63
　modeling, 64
　　system use cases, 65
　　use cases, 64
　nonfunctional requirements, 63
　reasons for using, 62-63
resources for learning more about
　　　UML, 215-217
risk management, 205-207
rolenames, 127
Rumbaugh, Jim, 2

S

scatter plot quadrants, 205
scope creep, 63
scoping use cases, 66-69, 72
sequence diagrams, 16, 80, 83-85
　application modeling, 133-135
　Business Analysis Model, 50-51, 53-54
　business analysis models, 175
　in UML 2.0, 196-197
signatures, 124
software architecture, 94
specifications, use cases, 80, 82
starting with UML, 204
state machine diagrams, 16, 188-190
statechart diagrams, 16, 188-190
states, 188-189
　nesting, 190
stereotypes, 99
　physical architecture, 104

substates, 190
subsystem tests, 169
  business analysis models, 174
subsystems, 99-100
Sun Microsystems, Core J2EE
    Patterns, 107
Sweet, William N., 166
synchronization points, 42
system architecture, 93-94
system level tests, 169
system use cases, modeling
    requirements, 65
systems, 99-100

T

teams
  apprenticeships, 210
  mentors, 209
  modeling teams, 210-211
  training traps, 208-209
  war rooms, 211-212
terminating activity, 42
testing, 165-166
  algorithmic testing, 178-179
  business analysis models, 173-176
  business use case models, 168-173
  class testing, 178-179
  database testing, 177
  examples, 166-167
  non-functional testing, 181
  performance testing, 181
  regression testing, 181
  unit testing, 177-179
timing diagrams, 17
training traps, examples of, 208-209
transitions, 189

U-V

UML (Unified Modeling Language), 2
  and object-oriented development, 4
  application modeling, 120
    class diagrams, 121-131
    sequence diagrams, 133-135
  business models, 33-35
  choosing designers, 207-208
  current events with, 6
  database modeling. *See* database
    modeling
  diagrams, 15-17
  interaction diagrams, 80
  origins of, 2-3
  proprietary, 3-4
  reasons for modeling with, 10-11
  what you can model, 12-13
  where to start, 204
UML 2.0, 193-194
  activity diagrams, 195
  class diagrams, 199-200
  collaboration diagrams, 194
  component diagrams, 197-198
  sequence diagrams, 196-197
UML analysis and design models, 177
  unit, class, and algorithmic testing,
    178-179
UML models, database modeling, 142, 144
  activity models, 146, 148
  class models, 148-149
  use case models, 145-146
Unified Method, 2
Unified Modeling Language (UML), 2
  and object-oriented development, 4
  application modeling, 120
    class diagrams, 121-131
    sequence diagrams, 133-135

business models, 33-35
choosing designers, 207-208
current events with, 6
database modeling. *See* database
    modeling
diagrams, 15-17
interaction diagrams, 80
origins of, 2-3
proprietary, 3-4
reasons for modeling with, 10-11
what you can model, 12-13
where to start, 204
unit testing, 177-179
United State Federal Government,
    enterprise architecture, 92
use case descriptions, 81-82
use case diagrams, 16
use case models
  Business Use Case Model, 35
    activity diagrams, 38-42, 44
    business use case diagram, 35-38
  database modeling, 145-146
use cases, 205-207
  actors, 72-75
  characteristics of, 65-70
  relationships, 75-79
  scoping, 66-69, 72
  sequence diagrams, 83-85
  specifications, 80, 82
  WAVE tests, 71

W

war rooms, 211-212
WAVE tests, use cases, 71
white box testing, 173

X-Y

XP (Extreme Programming), 14

Z

Zachman Framework, 93

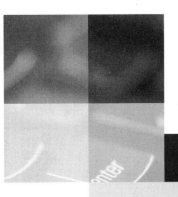